# Contents

① **Cake fundamentals**          01

The basics to making a cake from making the sponge to butter creaming and sugar pasting

② **Cakes for all occasions**          35

Cakes to WOW anyone. from a Christmas cake to a cereal milk cake there something to please everyone

③ **Baking**          55

Everything from Eaton mess to cheese and thyme scones this chapter has you covered for that quick and easy bake.

④ **Cookies**          75

From a classic chocolate chip cookie to the very best festive NYC cookie this chapter has your cookie dreams covered

⑤ **Traybakes**          98

One tin bakes all and in this section it real does. This section includes the like of a black forest brownie and a carrot cake traybake

⑥ **Cupcakes**          112

A simple cupcake can be turned into some of the most eye catching designs and flavours learn how in this chapter

⑥ **Cookie decorating**          151

Learn how to turn the most easiest sugar cookie recipe into the likes of baby vests and Easter eggs hand painted

⑥ **Celebration cakes**          176

Every cake needs a celebration and in this chapter I show you some of my favourite cake designs from a semi naked cake to a delicious hazelnut cake

⑥ **Children's baking**          190

Every child wants to bake so I have put together some of my fool proof children's recipes for this chapter.

## Equipment and Ingredients

- ☐ 250 g  margarine
- ☐ 250 g caster sugar
- ☐ 5 large eggs
- ☐ 250 g self raising flour

## Step 1

Preheat the oven to 170 degrees Celsius / 350 Fahrenheit/ gas mark 3 and grease and line 2 6 inch tins. Start by creaming the margarine and sugar together until light and fluffy. This should almost double in size. The longer you whip at this stage the lighter, fluffier your end sponge will be..

## Step 2

Next, mix in one egg at a time until all your eggs are full incorporated. If your mixture curdles, at any time, take one tablespoon of your flour and fold it through.

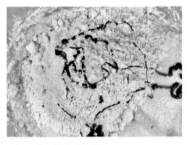

**Step 3**

*Next, add half your flour to your bowl and fold it through. Add the remaining half of your flour and your vanilla, remember to scrape the bottom of the bowl for any flour pockets that may be in the batter. Remember not to overmix the cake mix as you will activate your gluten in your cake.*

**Step 4**

*Next, line and grease your cake tins. I use a cake release spray. I also, add a circle of parchment paper to the bottom of my tin. I then, pour my cake mix into my lined tin and spread it out so its level.*

**Step 5**

*Bake in the oven for around 30-35 minutes or until a skewer comes out clean. Leave to cool in the tin for 15 minutes. If you take your cake out to soon it will shrink because of the temperature change. After 15 minutes, transfer to a cooling rack and allow to completely cool.*

## Tips

Never take your cakes out the tin to soon, else you will risk them shrinking due to the temperature change. Always make sure you use the best vanilla to maximise your flavour in your sponges, that is why I use little pod as it's the best fresh vanilla you can get, check out my vanilla recipe to make your own vanilla extract.

## Equipment and Ingredients

- ☐ 200 g caster sugar
- ☐ 200 g margarine
- ☐ 100 g milk chocolate
- ☐ 4 eggs
- ☐ 3 tbsp cocoa powder
- ☐ 3 tbsp boiling water
- ☐ 2 tbsp mayonnaise

**Decoration**
- ☐ 275  butter
- ☐ 450 g milk chocolate

## Step 1

Preheat the oven to 170 degrees Celsius / 350 Fahrenheit/ gas mark 3 and grease and line 2 6 inch tins.  Start, by whisking together your cocoa powder and eggs in a jug until you have no lumps. Set to one side to cool while we make the sponge batter.

## Step 2

Next, melt your butter and chocolate until fully melted. Be careful not to burn your chocolate. The quickest way to melt your butter and sugar is in the microwave, however you can do this in a bowl over some simmering water.

## Step 3

Next, fold through half your flour. Then fold through the other half of your flour, this ensures all your flour is fully incorporated. Then scrap down the mixture making sure there no flour pockets at the bottom of the bowl or ingredients not mixed in.

## Step 4

Finally, fold together your flour mixture, cocoa powder and egg mixture, sugar , mayonnaise and butter and chocolate mixture. Place into a two lined 6 inch tins. Bake for 40 - 50 minutes or until a cake tester comes out clean.

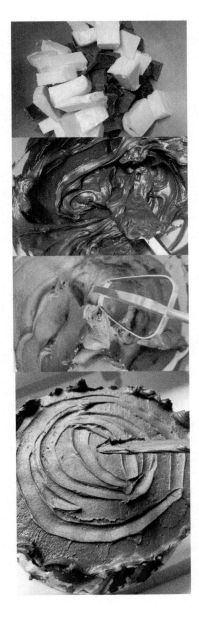

### Step 5

Whilst, your cakes are cooling melt you butter and chocolate. Be careful not to burn your chocolate. Set aside to firm up. Once firm, whip the ganache for 5 minutes until light and fluffy it will become lighter and almost the texture of buttercream.

### Step 6

Using a piping bag, pipe your whipped ganache into the middle of your cakes and smooth out using a pallet knife. Apply a generous amount of your whipped ganache to the side of the cake (the easiest way to do this is using a piping bag) then smooth out using a turntable and pallet knife or a side scraper for smoother sides. I then take a pallet knife and run it up with sides of the cake to make a almost like feather effect. I then run it around inwards on the top.

## Hints & tips

Use the best possible cocoa powder and not drinking chocolate for best results as drinking chocolate is a subtle flavour and isn't very nice to eat. If you do not want to add the mayonnaise, swap for golden syrup (mayonnaise is better as it gives you a moister richer chocolate cake) Just trust me!

## Equipment and Ingredients

- ☐ 175 g margarine
- ☐ 175 g caster sugar
- ☐ 3 eggs
- ☐ 275 g self raising flour
- ☐ 3 tbsp little pod coffee flavour
- ☐ 1 tbsp vanilla ( I use a little pod)
- ☐ 70 g walnuts

## Step 1

Start, by preheating your oven to 150 degrees/ 320 F/ gas mark 2 and line your loaf tin. Once your tin is lined, start whipping together your butter and sugar until light and fluffy, this will take around 5 minutes. You want to create lots of air as this is main process to give you a moist fluffy cake.

## Step 2

Next, add your eggs, flour, coffee flavouring, walnuts and vanilla. Mix all the ingredients until they are incorporated. Spoon the cake batter into your lined loaf tray and bake for 1 hour or until a cake tester or skewer comes out clean.

## Step 3

Once this has came out the oven, I mix up a batch of my buttercream and add 3 tbsp of coffee. I then, spread this over the top of the loaf (with a pallet knife) and finish with some chopped walnuts.

Throughout this book, I mention oven temperatures but as we all know everyone has different ovens from single ovens to double ovens to home ovens to commercial ovens. Therefore, the temperatures of the ovens differ so the best thing you can buy is an oven thermometer. An oven thermometer, tells you the exact temperature of the oven. Another factor that differs from each other regarding the oven could be the age as a newer oven is most likely to be correct and the exact temperature whereas another oven could be hotter if your fan isn't working or colder if you have a gap in your oven seal.

Another item that can affect your cakes and bakes, is your cake tins as you can imagine there are all brands of cake tins and with that comes some problems with which cake tins to get. I always recommended getting yours from a quality cake company rather than a cheap shop as we all know when we go to cheaper shops there can be many problems. For example, with the cheap shops the tins can sometimes not true to size, e.g. some tins are 7.9inches when they are supposed to be 8"inches and as we use more than one tin to bake our cakes this means some cakes are bigger and smaller than others. Also, you have the problem of them shrinking. I also do only recommend, not using silicone cake tins as if there knocked or moved against something when cooling they move to that shape and can move to different shapes. The solution to this problem, is to use the best cake tins you can get hold of like PME cake tins.

In each recipe, I call for ingredients that may be stored in the fridge (for example butter), but it is key to bring them to room temperature before you start using them, else the batter will curdle and your ingredients will struggle to combine. I always recommend, bringing ingredients out at least 30 minutes before you start baking so they have time to come up to room temperature. There is only one exception, when it comes to room-temperature ingredients and that is when we are making pastry of any type keep the ingredients out for as long as possible to keep  the buttery layers in the pastry.

With all my recipes and cakes, I must grease and line the tin to do this I use a product called release a cake and greaseproof paper. I find these the best way to slide my cakes out the tins and within this book I show you how to line your tins.

Another reason you could have problems baking, is that most people like to keep on opening the oven door and bang it shut all the time. There is no issue opening your door (except choux pastry) but you must shut it with care as else your bakes have a sudden temperature change and  will just sink. I always shut my door slowly, but if the top cake is done before the bottom shelf cake I will get it out without any problems as long as I shut the door carefully so the cake that isn't ready doesn't have a sudden temperature change.

The best investment you will ever have is, a set of electric scales and measuring spoons! As we all know, it can be simple to make errors and the most common errors come from not weighing out your ingredients properly. We all know a teaspoon right? But it isn't a technical measuring teaspoon meaning you could get a level teaspoon or a heaped teaspoon but if you invest in a cheap set of measuring spoons you accurately know you put an exact level teaspoon in the recipe. Also, some bakers go over by 50 grams and say that's ok or eyeball the weights but this is not accurate and can affect your recipe if you get your measurement wrong. It could make your cake batter too dry or too wet resulting in a bad cake.

Last but not least, my top tip for baking is to get prepared as we have all done it where we want to make a cake quickly and run around the kitchen following a recipe, then we can find out we do not have ingredients in or we forget to add something to the bake. Also, remember your cakes will need time to chill in-between baking and decorating, so make sure you make your cakes ahead of time (you can make them two days ahead of decorating). Before I get started, I like to weigh out all my ingredients into small bowls and make sure I have everything ready to go, for example, if I am using oranges I want them grated before I start making the curd for the filling.

Finally, I always say this to everyone do not bake when you are sad or angry , because I do not know why but your bakes can sense you are not happy and sheds a tear and will not be these gorgeous, delicious beautiful bakes you know they are.

Greasing and lining your cake tins is crucial to getting your cakes out to the tin. Do you have cakes that come away from the tins but some of the cakes still in the tin? Do you have cakes that just do not come out the tin? Well look no further, with these simple steps you can be making your cakes glide out the tin in seconds.

## Method 1

Start, by taking a piece of grease proof paper (this is optional) and take your margarine (I use Bako group cake margarine) grease the paper in butter and then wipe this around your tin. This should then, turn your tin shiny and forms grease film meaning you haven't left any out.

Next, take your sieved flour (I use carr's or wrights flour) either plain or self- raising will work. Then, place a tablespoon into your cake tins and using your hands turn the flour round the tin until evenly coated. You can now add your cake batter and bake.

## Method 2

Another way to grease and line your cake tins is, to take a greaseproof paper circle and place this into the bottom of your cake tin.

After you have your liner on the bottom of your tin, take a release a cake spray and spray the sides of the tin with the spray.

## Equipment and Ingredients

| | |
|---|---|
| 300 g caster sugar<br>260 ml double cream<br>100 ml water<br>1 tsp vanilla (optional)<br>pinch of salt (optional) | A large pan<br>A pastry brush<br>A spatula<br>A sterile jar |

**Step 1**

Start, by placing your sugar into a large heavy base sauce pan and pour over your water ensuring all your sugar is covered. Do not stir! Place on a low heat until your sugar dissolves.

**Step 2**

Once your sugar is dissolved, turn the heat up to a medium heat and bring the caramel to a amber colour. This will take about 5 minutes. Once your mixture starts to turn amber, don't walk away as it will change from being amber to being burnt quickly.

**Step 3**

Take your sugar and water mixture of heat and pour in a splash of your double cream at a time. It will bubble and steam so keep your hands away. Then, mix in the remaining cream. If you wish you can add salt or vanilla at this stage. Also, if you have any lumps place over a low heat to dissolve. Allow to cool before placing into your sterile jar.

## Hints & tips

When making caramel, make sure all your ingredients are ready. As you do not want to be leaving your caramel at any point as it is VERY HOT! Do not stir your mixture before adding your cream. Using a silicone spatula when stirring your caramel will make your life easier when washing up as the caramel comes of silicone easier. When cleaning up your use caramel equipment, soak in boiling water to melt the caramel off. Most of all be careful as when making caramel it get VERY HOT and can BURN you!

## Equipment and Ingredients

| | |
|---|---|
| Juice and zest of 5 lemons<br>4 eggs + 1 egg yolk<br>150 g caster sugar<br>75 g cold butter | A large pan<br>A bowl<br>A spatula<br>A sterile jar<br>A zester and juicer |

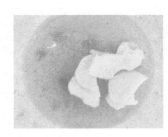

### Step 1

*Start, by melting your butter over a low heat. Once you have melted your butter, place it in a large bowl with your sugar, eggs and lemon juice and zest. Place the large bowl over a pan of simmering water and stir continuously.*

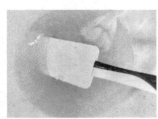

### Step 2

*Stir the mixture for 20-23 minutes continuously, until it thickens and when you coat a back of a spoon it does run of the spoon. Place a layer of clingfilm over the top of your curd and allow to cool before transferring to a sterilised jar.*

## Hints & tips

Lemon curd, orange curd, mango curd all the curds! You can swap the oranges for any fruit you wish. Make sure to keep clingfilm over your curds to stop a skin from forming over them. However, if a skin does form you can just scrap it off the top. Once your butter is melted you must not stop stirring else you could end up with scrambled eggs. If you are using smaller or larger oranges or different fruits do not worry still use the same quantities it will not affect the recipe.

## Equipment and Ingredients

| | |
|---|---|
| 200 g fresh fruit<br>200 g caster sugar or jam sugar<br>10 ml water | A large pan<br>A spatula<br>A sterile jar |

**Step 1**

*Start, by placing your fresh fruit with your water into into a large saucepan and slowly simmer over a low heat until they become soft and start to break down.*

**Step 2**

*Once your fruit is soft and starts to break down, pour over your sugar and turn up to a medium heat and allow to slowly boil.*

**Step 3**

*Once your fruit and sugar are boiling, reduce to a simmer and allow to simmer for 5 minutes. The sugar should dissolve and the fruit should shrink. Allow to cool before placing in a sterile air tight jar. If you don't want your Jam to have chunks of fruit you can use a potatoes masher to mash them down then strain them through sieve.*

## Hints & tips

When making homemade jam, always buy the fruit as close to making and using the jam as possible. The ratios are equal parts of fruit to sugar you can always making smaller or larger quantities. When storing your jam, always make sure your jam jars are sterile and air tight. If you are using caster sugar, remember your jam doesn't have any preservatives so won't last as long as using a jam sugar.

## Equipment and Ingredients

| | |
|---|---|
| 700 ml vodka<br>6 vanilla pods ( I use Little pod as they are the freshest and best) | A large pan<br>A spatula<br>A steriial jar |

### Step 1

*Start, by placing your vodka in a sterile jar. I the cut my vanilla pods in half and pop in the vodka. Leave in a dark, cool room for 6 months. the longer you leave it the better the vanilla.*

### Step 2

*Start, by placing your vodka in a small saucepan (make sure you have the lid). Slice your vanilla and boil the vanilla and vodka for 25 minutes or until a lovely vanilla colour.*

### Step 3

*Place you sliced vanilla into your vodka and then into a slow cooker halfway full up the side of the Jar with water. Slow cook for one hour. The colour should be very dark ad look intense.*

## Hints & tips

When making homemade vanilla, always buy the best vanilla pods you can I could not recommend Little pods vanilla pods any more as it makes delicious homemade vanilla. When storing your vanilla, always make sure your jam jars are sterile and air tight.  The better the vodka tastes the better your vanilla tastes is a rule I use.

## Equipment

- A cake (any size)
- A cake leveller or carving knife
- A turntable (if using a knife)

Start, by placing you cake onto a level side and using the nobs on the cake leveller to adjust to the height you want your cake. Next, take your cake leveller and go backwards and forwards through your cake until you have your cake leveller the whole way through the cake. Peel back the top of the cake, to revel your perfect layer of cake ready to fill and stack.

# Levelling with a knife

**Step 1**

Start, by placing your layer of cake on a turntable. (this will help you cut your cake even.

**Step 2**

Place your knife level with where you want to cut, then go around the cake spinning the turntable to make a mark. Once you have made a mark with the knife, lock you elbow and wrist and keep going round applying more pressure each time until your top layer slides off and your cakes with be even.

## Hints & tips

To level your cakes using a knife remember, to lock your hip and rotate your cake go in slowly don't cut it in one go. Always use a bread knife for best results. Do not do this on a turntable as you will struggle.

## Equipment and Ingredients

| | |
|---|---|
| 250 g butter | A bowl |
| 500 g icing sugar | A spatula |
| 2 tsp vanilla - I use Little pod | |

**Step 1**  Start, by whipping your butter on a high speed until it turns light and fluffy. This should take 6-7 minutes. The more you whip the lighter and whiter your buttercream will be.

**Step 2**  Sieve, your icing sugar. Then, fold the icing sugar through your butter to avoid an icing sugar cloud. Then, add in your vanilla and mix until the mixture comes together. This usually takes around 2 - 3 minutes.

## Hints & tips

If you want to make your buttercream chocolate flavoured or coloured, replace 50 grams of your Icing sugar with cocoa powder. If you want a pure white buttercream, you will need to add a whitener as your butter starts off yellow so adds a slight yellow hint to your buttercream. To change the flavour, simply take out the vanilla and swap it with your flavours. You can find a flavour supplier list in the back of this book. Do not forget to sieve the Icing sugar, as the icing sugar normally comes with lumps in it from where its been pressed down for packing.

## Equipment and Ingredients

| | |
|---|---|
| 800g of chocolate (milk, white or dark)<br>250ml double cream | A bowl<br>A spatula |

### Step 1

*Start, by pouring your double cream into a heavy base saucepan and bring the cream to a boil over a low heat. Do not rapidly boil else you will loose the texture and flavour of the cream.*

### Step 2

*While your cream is slowly boiling, place your chocolate into a plastic bowl. Once your cream is gently boiling, place the cream over the chocolate and allow to rest for 5 minutes.*

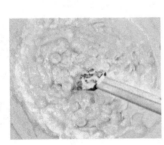

### Step 3

*Next, mix your mixture to combine the cream and chocolate. If there are left over chunks or chips of chocolate in your ganache, melt them in 10 second blasts in the microwave or over a double boiler stirring continuously until all the chips or chunks are gone.*

## Hints & tips

When making ganache, always use the best Belgium chocolate possible (I use Callebaut) as it will make your ganache taste better. Also, when using Belgium chocolate compared to value chocolate your ganache will have a higher chance of splitting as most value chocolate consist of vegetable fat instead of cocoa butter and oil and cream do not mix well. You can colour your ganache but only by using oil-based food colouring. If you use water-based colours your ganache will seize (You can tell when this has happened as your ganache forms a grainy, stiff texture).

## Equipment

- I patch of buttercream or softer ganache by adding 50-75ml more cream
- Your filling this can be anything from spreads to jams to caramels and curds
- A turntable

# Step 1

# Step 2

*Start, by filling your piping bag with your softer ganache or buttecream. Using your turntable to help you, pipe a dam of buttecream or ganache on the outside of your cake layer (Keep the turntable spinning and an event pressure on your piping bag for best results.)*

*Next, take your filling and place it into a piping bag and pipe your filling in the centre not over filling and using your dam as guide or if your filling got chunks or lumps, use a spoon and do not over fill your cake else your filling will leak down the side of your cakes.*

## Step 1

Start, by placing a blob of buttercream or ganache into the centre of your cake layer and use a pallet knife to evenly distribute your buttercream or ganache. Using a turntable and spinning evenly will help you get an even layer.

## Step 2

Using you pallet knife, press down in the centre (not holding you pallet knife allow over the cake just the centre)  spin your turntable and take out the centre until you see the cake layer come through. (it should look like the top of a semi naked wedding cake).

## Step 3

Once you have a crevice in the centre, use a spoon or piping bag and fill the centre just under the outside if you overfill you can will slide and will wobbly and if you are stacking them it could cause your tiers to collapse.

# Hints & tips

Do not add to much filling in the layers of your cake else they may go wonky and fall over. Always use a pallet knife to smooth over any fillings. If you add jam put buttercream around the sides and over the top to stop it spilling out the edges of the cake.

## Equipment and Ingredients

| 1 batch of simple buttercream: 250g butter 500 g icing sugar or ganache | A turntable<br>A spatula<br>A sharp edge smoother |
| --- | --- |

**Step 1** — Start, by placing your cake on a turntable and then apply a large amount of buttercream using the spatula around the sides of the cake. This will look messy and rustic but the more you add the easier it will be to become a smooth finished cake.

**Step 2** — Once you have your thick layer of buttercream or ganache, take your side scraper and spin around the cake to even out your coat of buttercream. If you have any holes or gaps apply more buttercream using a pallet knife.

**Step 3** — Apply a generous amount of buttercream to the top of your cake and then take your pro froster and spin. Once your cake is semi smooth, chill the cake in the fridge.

**Step 4** — After 15 minutes, take your cake out the fridge and place your right profroster in a bowl of boiling water and dry clean.

**Step 5** — Appling a small amount of pressure to your right angled smoother, spin your turntable evenly and this will smoother your cake. Remember not to apply to much pressure else you will scrap to much buttercream of but you can always reapply any butter cream.

## Equipment and Ingredients

| | |
|---|---|
| Sugar paste use my sugar paste size guide above for your size cake | A spatula<br>NYC cake sharp edge smoother<br>Side smoother<br>Squires kitchen flexi smoothers<br>Rolling pin |
| DO NOT SUGARPASTE YOUR CAKES ON A TURNTABLE!! | |

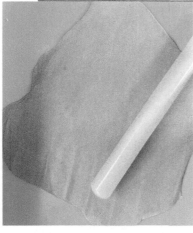

**Step 1**

Start, by rolling out your sugar paste or in this case I am using Squires kitchen cocoa form to around 3 - 4 mm thick you thicker you go the more chance of your sugar paste or cocoa form of ripping but the thinner you go the more chance you have of ripping as well that why 3 - 4 mm is a good thickness

**Step 2**

Take your rolling pin and fold your sugar paste or cocoa form over it. Take your rolling pin and place it over the cake to attach the sugar paste or cocoa form. Be careful not to pull your sugar paste or cocoa form with the rolling pin at the end. Also do not drop your rolling pin with the sugar paste as the impact of the rolling pin will cause your sugar paste to tear.

**Step 3**

Focusing on the top edge, take your sugar paste or cocoa form and rub your hands across it to secure your top edge. Now you top edge is secure you have limited any tears on your top edge. Finally go down and attach all the sugar paste or cocoa form by rubbing your hands down the cake.

**Step 4**

Finish by taking your smoother and applying pressure and rubbing it up and down this will attach your sugar paste to the cake. Sugar paste and cooca form will streach if you tease it do not poull else it will rip the easiest way is by rubbit it with the parm of your hand.

**Step 5**

Take your NYC sharp edge smoother and rub it side to side across your top edge. Finish by using the Squires kitchen flexi smoothers and rubbing them around the cake to smooth of any lumps or bumps.

## Equipment and Ingredients

If you are creating a two tiered cake or more you need the perfect structure. If you do not have the perfect structure, your cakes could bulge out and course a total mess, so in this section I give you my way of doweling and stacking a cake. Please remember to follow my dowelling chart for your size cakes. Also remember I do not use a central dowel system as I travel my tier dissembled and stack at the venue. There are so many dowels out there that are easy and accessible to everyone. Your question may be what dowels shall I use wooden or plastic shall they have a whole through the centre or not. My answer is yes they can be wooden all plastic and can have a whole in the centre it honestly does not matter all dowels will work and support your cakes to stop them collapsing on you. In this tutorial you will see that I use plastic but that because my local cake shop had them in stock.

### Step 1

To dowel your cake, start by taking a cake board the size of your top tier and making sure it is central by using a ruler and making sure you have the same gap all the way round the edge. Using a dresden tool, mark your central cake board and remove. Repeat for all tiers.

### Step 2

Once you have the cakes, push your dowels into the top of the cake and mark the bottom of the dowel with an edible pen. Then, cut the dowels using a pair of scissors or dowel cutter.

### Step 3

Once cut, simply insert into each cake and the place the tier on top of the tier below. Do not add dowels to our top tier.

## Equipment and Ingredients

| | |
|---|---|
| Sugarpaste<br>Edible glue or water | A Cake board<br>A rolling pin<br>A cake smoother<br>A paint brush |

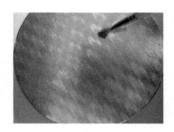

### Step 1

*Start, by using your paint brush and dipping it into your edible glue and water and brushing over your cake board. Set aside to allow to go tacky.*

### Step 2

*Roll out your sugar paste to around 3-5mm thick. Use the rolling pin to pick up your sugar paste and drape over your board making sure you do not crease the board.*

### Step 3

*Use your smoother to smooth out the sugar paste. Do not apply to much pressure else it will leave marks.*

# Hints & tips

Always roll out your sugar paste to 3-5 mm thick else you will see your board and it could crack if any thinner. Do not forget to go over with a smoother to flatten andy lumps or bumbs. I use blue fondant in the photo but you can use any other fondant colour you wish.

## Equipment and Ingredients

There are many dusts out there in matt colours and lustre colours. I know when you're getting started you think you need every brand of dust on the market but the truth is that you don't as almost every brand of dust has the same tones but they name them different. This is a way of costumers thinking there different from other brands but the truth is that there not they are the same tones just all brands have there own names for the tones.

When you buy dusts, you must look out for edible dusts, non edible and food contact. Edible means there safe to eat. Non edible means there not safe to eat. Food contact means that it can come into contact with food but must not be eat.

Brands do not tell you this, but with your left over dust you can let it evaporate then use a paint brush to scrape the dust and then all your left over paints can be reused and tipped back into your pot. With your left over paint you may not think there is a lot of dust left but once you allow it to dry and scrap it there is quite a bit of dust left.

Another top tip, is if your sugar paste has set firm and your dry dust isn't applying steam your cakes with a cake steamer or hot kettle water and then apply your dry dust. This allows your sugar paste to go soft and bond your dust. If your using it as a paint you will not need to do this set as your liquid will be your bonding agent instead of your sugar paste.

When you order your dust, either colour dusts or lustre dusts remember to check the net weight as some companies give you a estimated weight and fill the pot to the top but some companies say for example 7g and then fill the pot with 7g and it looks half full. But remember this comes down to density as some dusts are light and fluffy and would make that tub look full but then others would be compacted and make it look half full. Remember this if you're unsure always weighs what you have and check you have the weight you paid for.

Now let's get into colour dusts vs. lustre dusts. Colour dusts will give you a matte finish and give you full colour wear as lustre dusts will be twinkly and mainly your premium colours such as bronze and gold.

Sparkles will bling your cake but won't be bright it should just catch in the light remember if they are very bright and bold I would recommend check if they are edible as they are most likely not edible, however magic sparkle are very bright and completely edible.

# Cakes for all occasions

In this chapter you will see some of my favourite cakes that I have all year round from the family having dinner in to the Christmas cake at my table, I am sure there something for everyone in this chapter

## Equipment and Ingredients

- ☐ 175 g butter (not margarine)
- ☐ 175 g caster sugar
- ☐ 4 large eggs
- ☐ 250 g self raising flour (I use either car's flour or wright's bakes flour)
- ☐ Zest of 1 lemon or orange
- ☐ 1 tbsp vanilla ( I use little pod
- ☐ 4 tbsp milk (semi - skimmed or full fat)
- ☐ 1kg mixed fruit

500 g marzipan

1 pack of squires kitchen royal icing

## Step 1

Preheat the oven to 170 degrees Celsius / 350 Fahrenheit/ gas mark 3 and grease and lining an 8 inch square cake tin and boiling your mixed fruit in your alcohol or tea this will take about 5 minutes. Start by whipping your butter and sugar until light and fluffy,

## Step 2

Next, add your eggs, flour, both zests, mixed spice and vanilla. Mix on a high speed, until all the ingredients are incorporated and the mixture comes together with no pockets of flour. This should take around 4 minutes.

## Step 3

Next, fold through your dried fruit, mixed peel and chocolate chips, ensure all these are evenly distributed throughout your mixture to ensure an even bake.

## Step 4

Finally, spoon your mixture into your prepared cake tin, this should come 3/4 of the way up your tin. Bake in the oven for 2 hour or until a cake tester or skewer inserted into the cake comes out clean.

### Step 5

Next, roll out your marzipan to 3mm - 4mm thick you can go thicker if you wish. Then place it over the top of your fruit cake and use a sharp edge smoother around the top of the cake.

### Step 6

Last but not least, pinch down the side edges together and cutting it with a knife. This will give you nice sharp edges.

### Step 7

Mix together one bag of 500g of squires kitchen royal icing according to the packet. Use a pallet knife to apply this and wiggle the pallet knife around to make a swirl effect. Finally, press the pallet knife down and bring it back up to create a spikey effect. Top with your Christmas toppers.

## Hints & tips

You can add and change to which every fruit you wish as long as you have the 1kg. You can just cover in marzipan and serve. You may leave your marzipan overnight, however I royal ice straight over as I prefer my marzipan soften.

## Equipment and Ingredients

- ☐ 200 g  margarine
- ☐ 200 g caster sugar
- ☐ 4 large eggs
- ☐ 130 g plain flour
- ☐ 1 tsp baking powder
- ☐ 75 g cocoa powder
- ☐ Glace cherries

**To decorate**

- ☐ 300 ml double cream
- ☐ 12 whole cherries
- ☐ 75 g cherry jam

## Step 1

Preheat the oven to 170 degrees Celsius / 350 Fahrenheit/ gas mark 3. Start, by combing the margarine and sugar together until light and fluffy. This should become light and pale.

## Step 2

Next, mix in all your eggs. If you mixture curdles, add a tablespoon of your flour. However, the mixture curdling not going to effect the bake.

## Step 3

*Next, fold through your flour, cocoa powder and glace cherries. Lastly, scrape the bowl to avoid any pockets of flour. I like to make all my cakes by hand so I do not overmix them or leave pockets of flour.*

## Step 4

*Next, pour your batter into your foil traybake tin, you do not need to line these as the cakes pop out when you cut the tin. Finally, bake for 30 - 35 minutes or until a skewer comes out clean. Allow to cool fully.*

## Step 5

*Whip the cream until thcik and holds it shape. This will take about 5 minutes. If you over whip your cream, you can bring it back by adding more double cream out your pot into it.*

## Step 6

*Finally, transfer your cream into a piping bag fitted with an open star piping tip. Pipe rosettes by starting in the centre and working your way out. Then, top half with cherry Jam or whole cherries*

# Hints & Tips

Change the cherries for blackberries or strawberries. Use buttercream if you wish instead of cream the cream just gives you a lighter overall cake. Do not overmix your cake when the cherries are in there as it may turn your cake into a red cake and look like red velvet. Make sure you test the cake with a cake tester or skewer to see if its cooked.

## Equipment and Ingredients

☐ 250 g margarine
☐ 250 g light-brown sugar
☐ 5 large eggs
☐ 250 g self raising flour
☐ 1 tbsp salted caramel flavouring
☐ 1 tsp vanilla

**To decorate**
☐ 250 g popcorn
☐ 1 batch of 'simple buttercream recipe'
☐ 50 g salted caramel sauce

# Step 1

Preheat the oven to 170 degrees Celsius / 350 Fahrenheit/ gas mark 3 and grease and lining an 8 inch square cake tin. Start, by mixing the margarine and light brown sugar together until light and fluffy.

# Step 2

Next, mix in all your eggs and flour, caramel flavouring and vanilla. Lastly, scrape the bowl to avoid any pockets of flour. Do not overmix the batter else your flour can make your cake go dense as it will activate your gluten.

### Step 3

*Next, line and grease your cake tins. I use oil or butter and greaseproof paper to the sides and bottom using my lining a cake tin guide. Once lined, I place the batter in and smooth it out so it is level. This cake will fill a 4" deep tin just more than 3/4 full.*

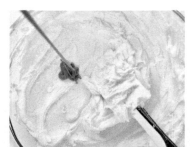

### Step 4

*Bake in the oven for around 30-35 minutes or until a skewer comes out clean. Leave to cool in the tin for around 15 minutes. This cake can come straight out the tin after 15 minutes and be left to cool on a wire rack. As we have used the light brown sugar, it gives the sponge a more dense structure (however it still delicious and moist to eat.)*

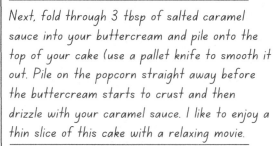

### Step 5

*Next, fold through 3 tbsp of salted caramel sauce into your buttercream and pile onto the top of your cake (use a pallet knife to smooth it out. Pile on the popcorn straight away before the buttercream starts to crust and then drizzle with your caramel sauce. I like to enjoy a thin slice of this cake with a relaxing movie.*

## Hints & Tips

You could add in your favourite chocolate inbetween the popcorn. Make a chocolate cake and have a drizzle of chocolate onto of the popcorn. Allow to cool fully before even making your buttercream as it will crust over in the time your waiting for your cake to cool.

## Equipment and Ingredients

- ☐ 250 g margarine
- ☐ 250 g light-brown sugar
- ☐ 4 large eggs
- ☐ 250 g self raising flour
- ☐ 150 g cornflakes
- ☐ 100 mls milk

**To decorate**

- ☐ 100 g cornflakes
- ☐ 1 batch of buttercream
- ☐ confetti sprinkles (I use scrumptious)

## Step 1

Start, by placing your cornflakes on a baking tray and bake them for around 15 minutes (they will toast up.) Then, pour your cornflake into your milk and set aside for 30 minutes. After 30 minutes, sieve our your cornflakes and it will leave you with cereal milk

## Step 2

After your cornflake milk is made, Preheat the oven to 170 degrees Celsius / 350 Fahrenheit/ gas mark 3 and grease and lining an 8 inch square cake tin we can start making our cake batter to do this I use an all in one method. Place your margarine, sugar, flour, eggs and 4 tbsp of cereal milk in a bowl and beat together until the mixture comes together (this can take a few moments).

### Step 3

*Next, line and grease your cake tins. I use oil or butter and paint it around the cake tin with a pastry brush and then apply a layer of greaseproof paper to the sides and bottom using my lining a cake tin guide. Once lined, I place the batter in and smooth it out so it is level. This will fill around half your 6 inch tin.*

### Step 4

*Bake in the oven for around 30-35 minutes or until a skewer comes out clean. Leave to cool in the tin for around 15 minutes. This cake can come straight out the tin after 15 minutes and be left to cool on a wire rack.*

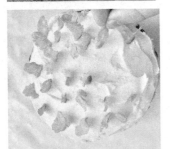

### Step 5

*Next, make a batch of my simple buttercream recipe and fold 3 tbsp of salted caramel flavouring. I then level my cakes using a cake leveller and cake leveller guide. I then, pipe the buttercream onto the bottom layer and add some of those cornflakes, then place the top layer. Then add some of the cornflakes to the side of your cake pushing them on with your hands. Last but not least, I pile on that buttercream on top of the cake and take some of the toasted cornflakes and stab them standing up into the cake. Finally, I sprinkle with some colourful sprinkles to give the cornflakes a real pop. I enjoy this cake with some custard or ice cream.*

## Hints & Tips

Do not over- toast your cornflakes as they can leave your bake with a burnt taste throughout.  If your buttercream is to soft leave it in the fridge and walk away and come back later on it will then spread like a dream. Once your flour is in your batter fold your mixture.

## Equipment and Ingredients

- ☐ 125 g butter
- ☐ 125 g lemon sugar
- ☐ 2 large eggs
- ☐ 125 g self raising flour
- ☐ 1 tbsp lemon flavouring

**To decorate**

- ☐ 100 g icing sugar
- ☐ water (not a perfect amount)
- ☐ 1 large lemon zest

# Step 1

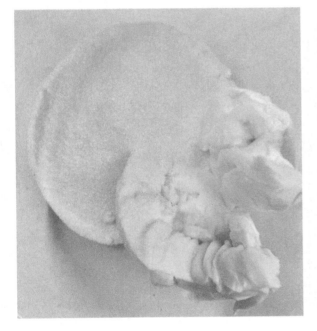

Preheat the oven to 170 degrees Celsius/ gas mark 3/ 320 Fahrenheit. Start, by placing your butter and sugar in a bowl and beating until it becomes light and fluffy. The sugar should of dissolved into the butter.

# Step 2

Next, fold through your eggs, flour and lemon flavouring. Make sure you scrape everything in your bowl so you do not have a pocket of lemon or a pocket of flour.

### Step 3

*Before you bake, all you need to do is place your batter into a mini loaf case and then place all your mini loafs onto a baking tray and bake for around 20 minutes or until a cake tester or skewer comes out clean. Allow to cool fully before decorating.*

### Step 4

*Once decorated brush with some lemon juice and sugar. This will create a sticky top on the mini lemon loafs.*

### Step 5

*Once fully cool, Let's decorate! To begin your decoration, add a tablespoon of water at a time into your icing sugar. Once fully incorporated, check the consistency so that there is a perfect amount. This is all done by eye and keep adding a tablespoon until you get to a runny icing but not opaque. Finish with the zest of lemon, and eat almost immediately for a sticky icing or leave for around 30 minutes if you want a cruncher icing.*

## Hints & Tips

If you icing is to runny I would thicken it up but if to thick add water to thin it down just want it to run controllably. When you zest your lemon, do this straight into the bowl to avoid wasting and of the juice or zest that comes of the lemon as this part has the most flavour

## Equipment and Ingredients

- [ ] 90 g butter
- [ ] 100 g light brown sugar
- [ ] 1 large eggs
- [ ] 125 g plain flour
- [ ] 175 g chocolate chips

**Edible cookie**

- [ ] 150 g butter
- [ ] 100 g of light brown sugar
- [ ] 70 g plain flour
- [ ] 40 g cocoa powder
- [ ] 75 g white chocolate chips

## Step 1

We make a simple cookie dough by beating you butter, sugar egg, flour, vanilla and chocolate chips until a paste is formed. Line 3, 6 inch cake tins.

## Step 2

Once you have your cookie dough, line two 6 inch tins and evenly spread your cookie dough into them. Preheat your oven to 170 degrees / 350 Fahrenheit and gas mark 3. Place you cookies in the fridge for 10 minutes to chill. Bake for 15 minutes or until golden brown.

## Step 3

*Allow your baked cookie dough to cool while we make a edible cookie dough to do this beat your butter, sugar, plain flour, cocoa powder and white chocolate chips until it forms a dough then place into another lined 6 inch tin. freeze for 1 hour, however leave a small amount and roll into balls and freeze them with cookie.*

## Step 4

*Take your batch of my simple buttercream and place it into a pipping bag fitted with an open star tip. Pipe over the bottom layer of your icing. pressing down and lifting up leave some space from the top edge as the weight of the cookie dough will push it down. Now add your frozen layer and repeat.*

## Step 5

*Pipe Mr Whippys, but every 45 degrees rotate. Do this by going round in a circular motion then carry on rotating up around about 3cm and flicking off at the top. Pipe around about 2.5cm wide . Then top with those cookie balls.*

# Hints & Tips

You could do the layer in the middle as a normal baked cookie by using the baking method just changing 75 g of flour with cocoa powder. Why not add white chocolate chips into the milk chocolate layer. Be carefull when baking a large cookie as it may be right in the middle so make sure it cooked by using a cake tester or skewer.

# Baking

In this chapter you will see some quick easy deserts from my millionaires tart to my cheese and time scones. This is the section to go to if your in a rush and want to treat someone tat last minute.

## Equipment and Ingredients

☐ 14 biscuits
☐ 120 g butter
☐ 100 ml double cream
☐ 200 ml milk chocolate
☐ 150 g caramel sauce (50 g for decoration

**To decorate**
☐ 200 mls double cream
☐ Fudge pieces

## Step 1

To begin this tart, melt your butter (you can add it to a saucepan and gradually heat it or shot bursts in the microwave.) While the butter is melting, I crush up my biscuits into irregular sized crumbs.

## Step 2

Once my biscuits are crushed and my butter is melted, mix them together to make a wet sand consistency which when pressed together holds it shape. Then tip it into my tart tin and use a measuring cup to compact the mixture into the tin and chill for I hour in the fridge.

## Step 3

Once the base is chilled, melt together your cream and chocolate and leave to one side for 5 minutes. After 5 minutes, stir until all the chocolate is melted. If there any chocolate lumps left, place over a double boil to melt them down. (You can do this by placing the chocolate and cream in the microwave until the chocolate melted.)

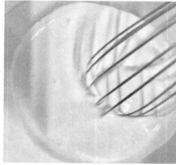

## Step 4

Take your ganache and pour over your base. Last but not least, allow to slightly firm up before using a piping bag to pipe in pockets of your caramel sauce. Use the sauce that comes to the top to marble the ganache and caramel together.

## Step 5

Finally, whip up your decorating cream until firm and stiff peaks form. Then transfer to a piping bag with a open start piping nozzle and pipe mini Mr Whippies by applying pressure and lifting up. Finish with a drizzle of caramel and fudge pieces.

## Hints & Tips

Make sure your tin is loose bottom else you will struggle to get your tart out. Do not allow your chocolate ganache mixture to start setting before pouring into the tin as you will find it tricky to smooth out.

## Equipment and Ingredients

- ☐ 175 g plain flour
- ☐ 85 g butter
- ☐ 2 - 4 tbsp water
- ☐ 150 g jam (of you flavour)
- ☐ 75 g butter

- ☐ 30 g light brown sugar
- ☐ 150 ml golden syrup
- ☐ 125 g cornflakes
- ☐ Magic Sparkles

## Step 1

Start, by making a quick and easy shortcrust pastry to do this place your flour in a bowl and rubber it together with your butter. This should make a crumble mixture. Then add water a tbsp at a time until the dough comes together to form one ball. Then refrigerate for 30 minutes

## Step 2

Once you have chilled your dough, preheat your oven to 180c/ Gas mark 4/ 350F.  Before, rolling your pastry to around 12 inches diameter. Wrap over your rolling pin and roll into your tin. Place your greaseproof paper in the tin and fill with baking beans or rice. Bake for 10 minutes before removing the rice/baking beans and baking for a further 5 minutes until golden brown.

### Step 3

Once baked allow to cool. Once cooled, fill around 1/4 of your tin with your jam. Place this in the fridge (while you make the cornflake mix) to set so you do not full any of your jam into your cornflake mix.

### Step 4

To make the cornflake mix, take your butter and golden syrup and melt them to make them runny. Tip your cornflake into a bowl and mix together the golden syrup and butter mix.

### Step 5

Take your jammy cornflake tart out the fridge and pile on the cornflake mix this will have a small dome on top. Finally, finish with some sparkles as everything looks better with sparkles.

## Hints & Tips

Once you pastry in the tin, remember to blind back because you do not want a soggy bottom. Once you have added your cornflakes allow to cool before setting in the fridge. You could use other jams such as raspberry or cherry.

## Equipment and Ingredients

- ☐ 14 digestive biscuits
- ☐ 120 g melted butter
- ☐ 300 g double cream
- ☐ 450 g cream cheese
- ☐ 150 g icing sugar

- ☐ 2 tbsp cappicouno flavouring
- ☐ 300 ml double cream
- ☐ Sweet stamp Carmel sauce
- ☐ 100g chocolate chips
- ☐ 100 g fudge pieces

## Step 1

Start, melting your butter, you can do this in the microwave or in a saucepan. Then crush the digestive biscuits very fine using a rolling pin and a zip lock bag.

## Step 2

Once, you have crushed my biscuits an melted my butter you combine them together to make a wet sand consistency. Then, use a tablespoon and add one tablespoon to each cupcake case and finely compact with a table spoon. Then, chill in the fridge.

**Step 3**

*While the biscuit base is chilling, make the filling, to do this whip the double cream and then add in then cappacunio flavouring and cream cheese and whip again until it gets to dropping concicentcy (where it slowly drops of the spatula)*

**Step 4**

*Once you have the cheesecake filling, fill the cupcake cases that already have the base and smooth them of with a tablespoon. Finally, freeze for 2 hours or refrigerate for 6 hours.*

**Step 5**

*Finally, whip up some cream (to stiff peaks) and fill a piping bag with the whipped cream (fill the piping bag with an open star piping tip, use Sweet stamp piping tips. Then pipe a MR whippy style by going around the outside and working my way in until you have a mountain of cream. Top with Sweet stamp caramel sauce, fudge pieces and chocolate chip*

## Tips

I make mini millionaire cheesecakes but you could make any flavour you want. The key for the cheesecake being stable is making sure you whip it until it hold it self when on a spatula. I make mine in cupcake cases but you could make a large one in a loose bottom tin.

## Equipment and Ingredients

- ☐ 300 g self-raising flour
- ☐ 1 tbsp baking powder
- ☐ 80 g butter (not margarine)
- ☐ 4 tbsp caster sugar
- ☐ 150 ml milk
- ☐ 1 tsp vanilla
- ☐ jam and clotted cream for serving

## Step 1

Add the butter (cubed) flour and sugar to a bowl and run in-between your fingers until they create a fine breadcrumb. If the butter starts melting place, place it in the fridge for 10 minutes and come back so that the butter firms up.

## Step 2

Next, add your milk, vanilla and baking powder (do not add the baking before else your scones will be tough as you will have activated the gluten) and mix until it forms a dough.

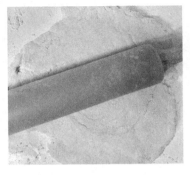

## Step 3

*Take your dough and tip onto a floured work-surface and roll out to roughly 3 - 4 cm deep take your circle cutters and dip in flour and cut out your scones (I use purple cupcakes circle cutters)*

## Step 4

*Place onto a lined baking tray and brush with a beaten egg or some milk (to stop them from burning) and bake for 10-12 minutes or until they have a nice golden touch and have a nice rise.*

## Step 5

*Then, fill with your Jam and cream. You can do this jam first or cream first I do jam first then cream but it is up to you.*

## Hints & Tips

Once you made your scones, the trick is to not over knead them. Once you cut them once the second ones won't rise as much ect and you will have a chewy scone. You could add some raising or chocolate chips if you wish. You want to make sure you put the am on first else your jam would fall down the side of the cream. Debate over Jam then cream.

## Equipment and Ingredients

- ☐ 300 g self-raising flour
- ☐ 1 tbsp baking powder
- ☐ 80 g butter (not margarine)
- ☐ 4 tbsp caster sugar
- ☐ 150 ml milk
- ☐ 150 g of cheese (use the best quality you can find)
- ☐ 3 tbsp of thyme you can use fresh

## Step 1

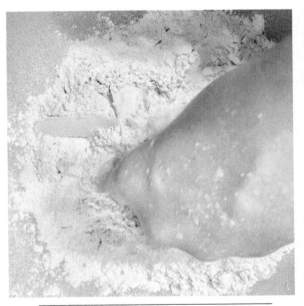

Add the butter (cubed) flour and sugar to a bowl and run in-between your fingers until they create a fine breadcrumb. If the butter starts melting place, place it in the fridge for 10 minutes and come back so that the butter firms up.

## Step 2

Next, add your milk, vanilla, thyme and cheese (leave a handful of cheese behind) and baking powder. Mix these in by cutting through the bread crumbs.

**Step 3**

Take your dough and tip onto a floured work-surface (I use my non-stick green board) and roll out to roughly 3 - 4 cm deep take your circle cutters and dip in flour and cut out your scones (I use purple cupcakes circle cutters)

**Step 4**

Place onto a lined baking tray and brush with a beaten egg or some milk and top with the left over cheese and bake for 10-12 minutes or until they have a nice golden touch and have a nice rise. I then cut mine and serve with butter.

# Hints & Tips

The trick is not to melt your butter with these scones. Once you have made your first, cut out the second or it will not rise or look as good and this continues as the butter will start to melt on the inside and this helps the scones rise.

## Equipment and Ingredients

- ☐ 600 g milk chocolate
- ☐ 150 g scrumptious chocolate mini eggs
- ☐ 300 g Digestive biscuit (crushed)
- ☐ 60 g butter (melted)
- ☐ Magic Sparkles

# Step 1

Start by melting you chocolate (you do not need to temper for this recipe) and place it in a large bowl with your crushed digestive biscuits, Scrumptious mini eggs and melted butter and fold it all together. It is simple as that for your chocolate biscuit cake recipe.

# Step 2

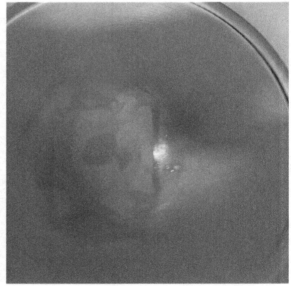

Grease a 1 litre Pyrex bowl and add greaseproof square to the bottom. Next, fill it with your chocolate biscuit cake and place a greaseproof paper on top to smooth out the base. Allow to set overnight in the fridge or a minimum of 4 hours

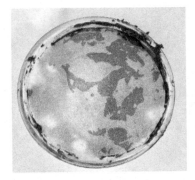

## Step 3

Take your chocolate biscuit cake and place it on a cake board. (I use Olbaa.) Then we can begin decorating into a Christmas pudding.

## Step 4

Start by rolling out some sugar paste to around 2 - 3mm thick and take your drippy icing cutter (A cake for you is the best as it give you clean edges and an exact shape.) and cut it out. (I use my green board to stop my sugar paste from sticking).

## Step 5

Use a little bit of water on the back of the sugar paste to stick onto the chocolate biscuit cake. You can also use edible glue to stick this on. Finish with some Dr oetker edible flowers

# Hints & Tips

The great thing with chocolate biscuit cake is you can add or take anything you want why not add some raisins or marshmallows. Do not try and release the chocolate biscuit cake out the bowl to soon as it won't come out or will come out in two halves as the chocolate sets it releases it self from the bowl.

# Cookies

My favourite chapter in the book! Cookies are a true classic bake in my house and with this section of the book it can surely be a true classic in your house. I include my new favourite festive cookie and my all time classic cookie chocolate chip.

## Equipment and Ingredients

- ☐ 150 g butter
- ☐ 150 g light brown sugar
- ☐ 1 egg
- ☐ 200 g self raising flour
- ☐ 175 g milk chocolate chips
- ☐ 1 tsp vanilla

## Step 1

Mix together your butter and sugar until combined, there is no need to cream else your cookies may spread out. You want it to form a light brown paste.

## Step 2

Next, fold in your egg and flour. You then want to mix this until you can no longer see any egg spots or flour pockets so it is fully incorporated. Do not overmix else your cookies may flatten when baked.

### Step 3

Once you have folded your flour and eggs, take your chocolate chips and fold them through until fully incorporated. At this stage, you want to then roll your cookies into 100 g balls and freeze for at least 2 hours ideally overnight.

### Step 4

Finally, place onto a lined baking tray and bake for 15 - 18 minutes or until golden brown. Then, top with a chunk of chocolate out the oven. You could always dip yours in chocolate if you leave them to cool.

## Hints & Tips

Change the chocolate from milk chocolate to white or dark chocolate. Remember, to freeze for best results. Do not overbeat or warm the mixture up as you do not want that butter to melt as that gives you all the texture.

## Equipment and Ingredients

- ☐ 230 g butter
- ☐ 200 g light brown sugar
- ☐ 100 g fudge pieces
- ☐ 200 g plain flour
- ☐ 1 tsp baking powder
- ☐ 400 g white chocolate chips
- ☐ 200 g chocolate chips
- ☐ 100 g caramelised biscuits
- ☐ 200 g of chopped nuts

- ☐ 1 tsp vanilla
- ☐ 500 g self - raising flour
- ☐ 2 whole eggs
- ☐ 100 g funfetti sprinkles

## Step 1

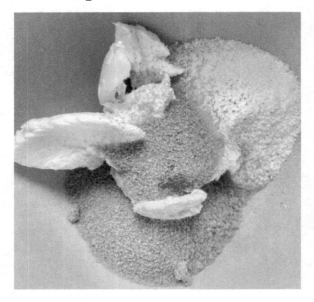

Mix together your butter and sugar until they form nuggets of butter and sugar. There should be chunky and irregular. Do not overmix else your cookies won't be chunky and gooey like a NYC cookie.

## Step 2

Next, add in your egg, flour, baking powder and vanilla. You then want to mix this until you can no longer see any pockets of egg or flour. Do not overmix else your cookies will flatten in the oven.

## Step 3

Once you have half folded your cookie, take your chocolate chips and fold them through until fully incorporated. At this stage, you want to then roll your cookies into 125 g balls and then roll your balls in your chopped nuts and freeze for at least 4 hours ideally overnight.

## Step 4

Finally, place onto a lined baking tray and bake for 12 - 15 minutes or until golden brown. I like to enjoy warm with a scoop of ice cream.

# Hints & Tips

You can add more of something or take something away if you do not like it. These cookies are a bit like a rocky road as they have a bit of everything in and you can add and change them. Do remember to freeze for 6 hours to help with that shape and texture of the cookie.

## Equipment and Ingredients

- ☐ 200 g butter
- ☐ 100 g light brown sugar
- ☐ 100 g caster sugar
- ☐ 200 g white chocolate chips
- ☐ 1 tsp vanilla
- ☐ 470 g self - raising flour
- ☐ 2 whole eggs
- ☐ 200 g lemon curd
- ☐ 4 meringue nests

## Step 1

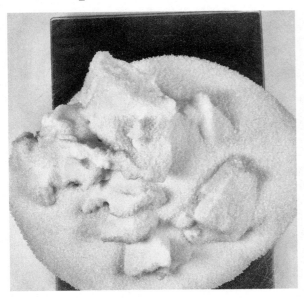

Start, by getting two tablespoons and creating blobs of lemon curd onto a baking tray or plate and freeze for 30 minutes until they are firm to touch and not pipeable.

## Step 2

Mix together your butter and sugar until they form nuggets of butter and sugar. There should be chunky irregular pieces of butter and sugar. Do not overmix else your cookies won't be chunky and gooey like a NYC cookie.

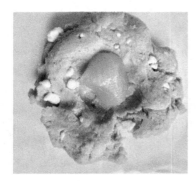

**Step 3**

*Next, add in your egg, flour, chocolate chips and meringue and vanilla. You want to mix this but not overmix as overmixing these cookies will make them flat. You should have no egg left pockets or flour pockets of your butter and sugar.*

**Step 4**

*At this stage, you want to then roll your cookies into balls, however before rolling the balls take your lemon curd and place them around the cookie and make sure they are encased. Once the dough has come together, roll the dough inbetween your hands to make loose chunky balls. Do not roll into perfect round balls else they will flatten out..*

**Step 5**

*Finally, place onto a lined baking tray and bake for 12 - 15 minutes or until golden brown. I like to enjoy warm with a scoop of ice cream.*

## Tips

Change your lemons for limes? Do not overmix your cookie dough else they will deflat. Always freeze for 6 hours minimum and this helps with that goey center and crisp outside shell.

## Equipment and Ingredients

- ☐ 200 g butter
- ☐ 200 g light brown sugar
- ☐ 200 g milk chocolate chips
- ☐ 200 g white chocolate chips
- ☐ 500 g self - raising flour
- ☐ 2 whole eggs
- ☐ 250 g caramelised biscuit spread
- ☐ 10 caramelised biscuits

## Step 1

Start, by taking two tablespoons caramelised sauce and creating blobs sauce onto a baking tray or plate and freeze for 30 minutes until they are firm to touch and not pipeable. Also mix together your butter and sugar until they form nuggets of butter and sugar. There should be chunky irregular pieces of butter and sugar. Do not overmix else your cookies won't be chunky and gooey like a NYC cookie.

## Step 2

Next, fold in your eggs, white chocolate (I use Squires Kitchen) and flour. You want to mix this but not overmix as overmixing these cookies will make them flat. You should have no pockets of egg or flour left.

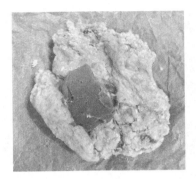

### Step 3

*At this stage, you want to then roll your cookies into balls, however before rolling the balls take your caramelised sauce and place them around the cookie and make sure they are encased. Once this is done rub the dough in between your hands to make loose chunky balls.*

### Step 4

*Finally, place onto a lined baking tray and bake for 12 - 15 minutes or until golden brown. Leave to cool on the baking tray.*

### Step 5

*Then, dip in caramelised spread and sprinkle with caramelised biscuit crumbs. Then, drizzle in white chocolate for and contrast in colour.*

## Hints &Tips

You can change your biscuits to a different biscuit. You could also use chocolate spread instead of caramelised spread. Remember to freeze before baking. Do not overmix your cookie dough as this can result in a flat cookie.

## Equipment and Ingredients

- ☐ 200 g butter
- ☐ 200 g light brown sugar
- ☐ 200 g self raising flour
- ☐ 200 g milk chocolate chips
- ☐ 200 g glace cherries
- ☐ 2 whole eggs

## Step 1

Mix together your butter and sugar until they form nuggets of butter and sugar. There should be chunky irregular pieces of butter and sugar. Do not overmix else your cookies won't be chunky and gooey like a NYC cookie.

## Step 2

Next, fold in your egg, flour and milk chocolate. You want to fold this but not overmix as overmixing these cookies will make them flat. You want to make sure all the ingredients are full incorporated.

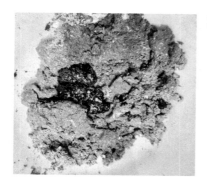

### Step 3

Once you have half folded your cookie, take your cherry jam and fold them through until fully incorporated. Do not overmix else you won't get your pockets of jam.

### Step 4

At this stage, you want to then roll your cookies into balls. Do not roll into tight balls you want them chunky and irregular. Freeze for 6 hours to give you that chunky cookie shape.

### Step 5

Finally, 15 minutes before you want to bake. When you want a cookie, Preheat your oven to 180 degrees Celsius / gas mark 3 / 350 degrees Fahrenheit. Place your cookies onto a lined baking tray and bake for 15 - 18 minutes or until golden brown. Leave to cool on the baking tray.

## Tips

Change the cherries for other fruits such as blackberries or raspberries. Do not over mix your batter else your cookies will be flat. Also, do not forget to freeze else your cookies will flatten out and the jam will cause a stick miss and that not what we want as that jam pools out this cookie once bitten into.

## Equipment and Ingredients

- ☐ 200 g butter
- ☐ 200 g light brown sugar
- ☐ 500 g self raising flour
- ☐ 300 g milk chocolate chips
- ☐ 75 g cocoa powder
- ☐ 3 tbsp of water
- ☐ 2 eggs

## Step 1

Mix together your butter and sugar until they form nuggets of butter and sugar. There should be chunky irregular pieces of butter and sugar. Do not overmix else your cookies won't be chunky and gooey like a NYC cookie.

## Step 2

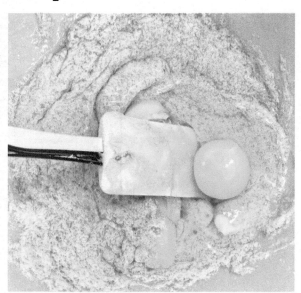

Next, add in your egg. You want to fold this in but not overmix as overmixing will make the cookies flatten when baked. You should have no egg left in pockets of your butter and sugar.

### Step 3

Once you have added your egg, you want to half-fold through your your flour until you are getting little bits of flour on the top. Do not mix at this stage only fold else you will activate the gluten in your flour and it will result in a chewy, tough cookie. And they will spread out once baked.

### Step 4

Once you have half folded your cookie, take both your chocolate chips and fold them through until fully incorporated. Do not overmix else your chocolate will melt.

### Step 5

Roughly split your batter into two bowls and to the one add your water and cocoa powder to make a double chocolate cookie. Leave the other one as it is.

### Step 6

At this stage, you want to then roll your cookies into balls. Take 50g of the double chocolate 50g of the single chocolate chip and roll them together. These balls can be rolled into smooth balls. Freeze for a minimum of 6 hours.

### Step 7

Finally, 15 minutes before you want to bake, preheat your oven to 180 degrees Celsius / gas mark 3 / 350 degrees Fahrenheit. Place your cookies onto a lined baking tray and bake for 15 - 18 minutes or until golden brown. Leave to cool on the baking tray.

## Hints & Tips

If you like one cookies more than the other you can add more of that cookie ie double chocolate over single chocolate. You could add white chocolate chips. Remember to freeze after you have rolled into balls else your cookies will be flat and very very chewy where these are suppose to be chunky and gooey and melt in the mouth

## Equipment and Ingredients

- ☐ 200 g butter
- ☐ 200 g light brown sugar
- ☐ 200 g milk chocolate chips
- ☐ 250 g mixed fruit
- ☐ 150 ml of tea or brandy
- ☐ 2 tbsp of mixed spice
- ☐ 500 g self - raising flour
- ☐ 2 whole eggs
- ☐ 150 g Marzipan (I use renshaw)

## Step 1

Start, by soaking your fruit in your tea or alcohol overnight or boil in a saucepan for around 1 hour and you are good to go just allow it to cool down before you start your cookies.

## Step 2

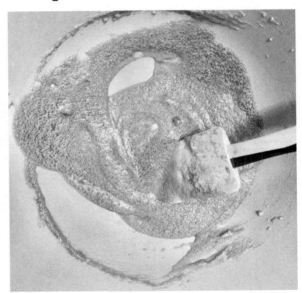

Mix together your butter and sugar until they form nuggets. There should be chunky irregular pieces of butter and sugar. Do not overmix else your cookies won't be chunky and gooey like a NYC cookie.

**Step 3**

*Next, add in your egg. You want to fold this but not overmix as overmixing these cookies will make them flat. You should have no egg left in pockets of your butter and sugar.*

*Once you have added your egg, you want to half-fold through your your flour and mixed spice until you are getting little bits of flour on the top. Do not mix at this stage only fold else you will activate the gluten in your flour and it will result in a chewy, tough cookie. And they will spread out once baked.*

**Step 4**

**Step 5**

*Once you have half folded your cookie, take your chocolate chips, mixed fruit and marzipan chunks fold them through until fully incorporated. Do not overmix else your chocolate will melt.*

*At this stage, you want to then roll your cookies into balls, however rub in between your hands to make loose chunky balls (go clunk clunk and they will be ready). Freeze for 6 hours or overnight.*

**Step 6**

**Step 7**

*Finally, 15 minutes before you want to bake preheat your oven to 180 degrees Celsius / gas mark 3 / 350 degrees Fahrenheit. Place your cookies onto a lined baking tray and bake for 15 - 18 minutes or until golden brown. Leave to cool on the baking tray.*

## Hints & Tips

You could leave things like the marzipan out or change from milk chocolate chips to the dark chocolate chips or eave the chocolate out. You could add your favourite fruit if there ones you don't like in the mixed pack.

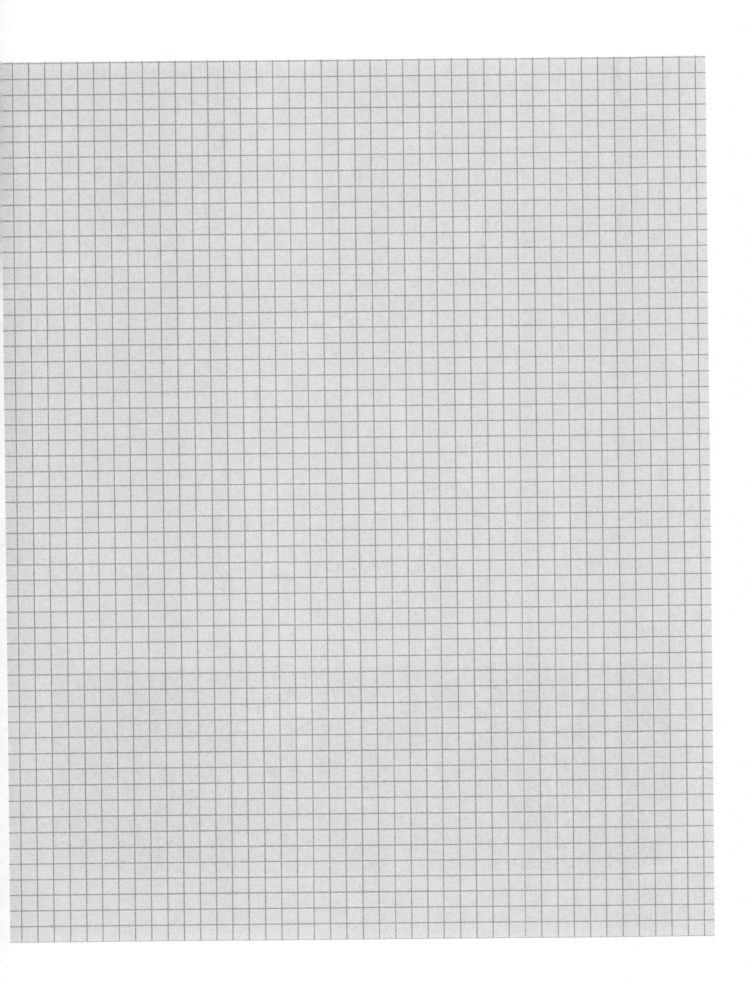

# Traybakes

This is my one tin bakes all chapter within this section all you need is a few ingredients and a bowl and a spoon plus one baking tin and you will be underway to creating delicious traybakes everytime.

## Equipment and Ingredients

- ☐ 175 g margarine
- ☐ 300 g light brown sugar
- ☐ 3 eggs
- ☐ 75 g plain flour
- ☐ 55 g cocoa powder
- ☐ 300 g milk chocolate
- ☐ 150 g caramelised biscuit spread
- ☐ 10 caramelised biscuits

## Step 1

Preheat the oven to 170 degrees Celsius / 350 Fahrenheit/ gas mark 3. Start, by melting together your chocolate and margarine. You can do this in a bain-marie (Saucepan of simmering water with a bowl over the top) or short burst in the microwave. While your mixture is melting whisk together your eggs and sugar until they become frothy this will make the crackly top on your brownies.

## Step 2

Once you have allowed your chocolate mixture to cool down and whisked your eggs, fold your egg mixture into your chocolate mixture. Remember to scrape the bottom of the bowl so both mixtures incorporate.

### Step 3

Once you have folded both mixture together fold through your flour. Do not mix or beat as all the air you created in your eggs will collapse and when baking the brownies will make them sink in the centre.

### Step 4

Finally, transfer to your brownie tray/tin. Once transferred get your caramelised biscuit spread and add dollops of this across your brownie and use a skewer or cake tester to swirl into your brownie. Finish with some crushed up caramelised biscuit crumbs.

### Step 5

Finally, transfer to the oven and bake for 25 - 30 minutes or until you have a slight wobble. If you want your brownies more cakey bake for a further 5 - 10 minutes (but honestly gooey brownies are the best)

## Hints & Tips

I use caramelised biscuits you could use cookies or any other biscuit. If you do not like the toasted biscuits on top you can add them half way through baking however I feel they add to the texture. Leave your brownie overnight in the fridge for a fudgier brownie.

## Equipment and Ingredients

- ☐ 175 g margarine
- ☐ 300 g light brown sugar
- ☐ 3 eggs
- ☐ 75 g plain flour
- ☐ 55 g cocoa powder
- ☐ 350 g dark chocolate
- ☐ 200 g glace cherries

## Step 1

Preheat the oven to 170 degrees Celsius / 350 Fahrenheit/ gas mark 3. Start, by melting together your margarine and 300 g of your dark chocolate. You can do this in a bain-marie (Saucepan of simmering water with a bowl over the top) or short burst in the microwave. Set aside and allow to cool down.

## Step 2

Next, add your eggs and sugar to a jug or bowl and whisk together for around 3 to 4 minutes while your chocolate and butter mixture is cooling down. The mixture should have a foam on the top and that is when you know it ready. This is the critical part to getting a crackle on your brownies.

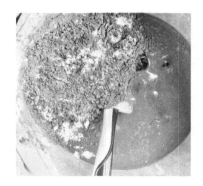

### Step 3

Once you have allowed your chocolate mixture to cool down and whisked your eggs, fold your egg mixture into your chocolate mixture. Remember to scrap the bottom of the bowl so both mixtures incorporate.

### Step 4

Once you have folded both mixture together fold through your flour. Do not mix or beat as all the air you created in your eggs will collapse and when baking the brownies will make them sink in the centre.

### Step 5

Finally, fold through your remaining dark chocolate and glace cherries. You do not want these to melt so it is best to do this at this stage.

### Step 6

Finally, transfer to your brownie tray/tin and bake for 30 - 35 minutes or until you have a slight wobble. If you want your brownies more cakey bake for a further 5 - 10 minutes (but honestly gooey brownies are the best)

## Hints & Tips

You need to be aware that once your cherries are in to keep the nice dark colour you do not want to mix as much as this will bleed and turn your cake red.  If you like your brownies fudgier leave in the fridge overnight before serving. Do not mix once your flour is in, else the air you created with the eggs will collapse and your brownies may sink.

## Equipment and Ingredients

- ☐ 100 g margarine
- ☐ 200 g caster sugar
- ☐ 2 eggs
- ☐ 70 g plain flour
- ☐ 60 cocoa powder
- ☐ 250 g caster sugar
- ☐ 160 ml double cream
- ☐ 80 g butter
- ☐ 175 g cornflakes

## Step 1

Preheat the oven to 170 degrees Celsius / 350 Fahrenheit/ gas mark 3. Start, by melting together your margarine and milk or dark chocolate. You can do this in a bain-marie (Saucepan of simmering water with a bowl over the top) or short burst in the microwave. While this mixture is melting whisk together you eggs and sugar until frothy this will give you the crackly top a brownie should have.

## Step 2

Once you have allowed your chocolate mixture to cool down and whisked your eggs, fold your egg mixture into your chocolate mixture. Remember to scrape the bottom of the bowl so both mixtures incorporate.

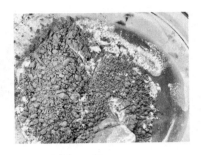

**Step 3**    Once you have folded both mixture together fold through your flour. Do not mix or beat as all the air you created in your eggs will collapse and when baking the brownies will make them sink in the centre.

**Step 4**    Finally, transfer to your brownie tray/tin and bake for 25 - 30 minutes or until you have a slight wobble. If you want your brownies more cakey bake for a further 5 - 10 minutes (but honestly gooey brownies are the best).

**Step 5**    Once your brownies are baked lets start making the carmel. To do this, boil your water and sugar over a low heat until it turns ambeer. Once turned amber pour over your cream and stir through your butter.

**Step 6**    Finally, to finish your cornflakes brownies pour over your cornflakes and then tip onto of your brownies and smooth out allow to chill overnight before cutting your a heated sharp knife.

## Hints & Tips

BE VERY CAREFUL WITH THE HOT CARAMEL!! You can change the cornflakes if you wish for other cereals. When mixing your batter, whisk your eggs untill foamy as this gives you the nice crackly top on the brownie. Always leave brownies overnight in the fridge before serving as they go even gooier.

## Equipment and Ingredients

- ☐ 125 ml oil
- ☐ 120 g light brown sugar
- ☐ 3 eggs
- ☐ 125 g self raising flour
- ☐ 1 tbsp cinnamon
- ☐ 1 tbsp ground ginger
- ☐ 250 g grated carrots
- ☐ 50 g walnuts

## Step 1

Preheat the oven to 170 degrees Celsius / 350 Fahrenheit/ gas mark 3. Start, by placing all your ingredients (oil, light-brown sugar, eggs, self- raising flour, cinnamon, ginger , carrots, walnuts) and mixing them together until combined. This mixture is not the best looking but is delicious and moist once baked.

## Step 2

Next, place your carrot cake mixture in your tin and smooth it out. (Use a pallet knife to smooth it out). Then bake for 50 minuities or until a skewer comes out clean. Allow to cool in your tin.

### Step 3

Once cool, begin making my cream cheese frosting to do this mix together the butter and cream cheese until combined and soft. Finally, fold through your icing sugar with a drop of vanilla. Do not be to concerned if your icing is not thick as this icing firms up in the fridge.

### Step 4

Once this is done, spread the cream cheese frosting over the top and then go over side to side with my pallet knife to give a pallet effect.

### Step 5

To top this traybake, use Dr Oetker white chocolate carrots and refrigerate overnight to help that icing firm up slightly.

## Hints & Tips

Make sure you giggle your cake tester around and move it around your tin as it can sometimes give you a false reading. If you do not feel confident it's baked the chances are it isn't so I would leave it another 10 to 15 minutes. You can make this cake in a round cake tin. Also, do not be to concerned if you cream cheese icing is a bit sloppy once first made as it will firm up in the fridge.

# Cupcakes

A small sponge cake which can be decorated in endless way and that is what il will show you in this chapter from my love is in the air cupcakes to my Halloween blood cupcakes there something for every season.

## Equipment and Ingredients

- ☐ 125 g margarine
- ☐ 125 g caster sugar
- ☐ 3 eggs
- ☐ 125 g self raising flour
- ☐ 1 tsp vanilla

## Step 1

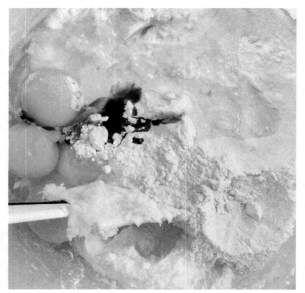

Preheat the oven to 170 degrees Celsius / 350 Fahrenheit/ gas mark 3. Start, by placing all your ingredients (margarine, flour, sugar and eggs) in a bowl and mix them together until combined. This mixture should holds its self but not be super stiff.

## Step 2

Next, use two teaspoons and place into your cupcake tin and bake for 25 - 30 minutes or until golden brown. A cake tester or skewer will come out clean once baked.

## Equipment and Ingredients

☐ 100 g margarine
☐ 150 g icing sugar
☐ 3 eggs
☐ 110 g self raising flour
☐ 1 tsp vanilla
☐ 25 g funfetti sprinkles

**Decoration**

☐ 200 g butter
☐ 550 g icing sugar
☐ 1 tsp vanilla
☐ 25 g funfetti sprinkles

## Step 1

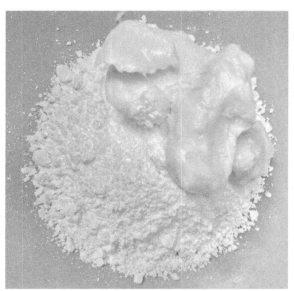

Preheat the oven to 170 degrees Celsius / 350 Fahrenheit/ gas mark 3. Start, by mixing your margarine and sugar until light and fluffy. Then mix in eggs and make sure they are fully incorporated. Make sure you fully fold all your eggs and scrape the bottom of your bowl.

## Step 2

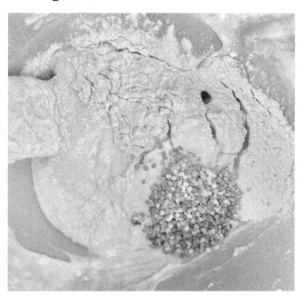

Finally, mix in your flour, vanilla and sprinkles. Make sure you do not overmix once you have added your sprinkles else they may blead into the batter. Next, spoon (or use an ice cream scoop) your cupcake batter into your cupcake cases. They could be around 3/4 full for the perfect cupcake. Bake for around 22 - 25 minutes or until golden brown

## Step 3

Once cool, I begin making my buttercream to do this I mix my butter until light and fluffy. Finally, fold through your icing sugar with a drop of vanilla. This should hold it self on a spatula and gradually fall of. If your buttercream is to stiff, add a tablespoon of liquid (ie milk or water) until it loosens up. It is the same the other way if it to soft add 50 g of icing sugar at a time until firm.

## Step 4

Once you have made your buttercream transfer it to a piping bag (fitted with an open star tip) and pipe Mr Whippy by going round the edge of my cupcake over lapping the last circling but not letting go of the pressure and when you are at the top flick of. Then, top mine with funffetti sprinkles.

## Hints & Tips

Make sure you fold through your sprinkles at the end, as if you add them with your eggs they will bleed into them and your cupcake batter will die a different colour and you will not have that funfetti effect. You can use pastel sprinkles or mermaid sprinkles or any other sprinkles if you wish. The icing sugar gives you a litter sponge so those sprinkles pop you can use caster sugar if you wish.

## Equipment and Ingredients

☐ 100 g margarine
☐ 150 g caster sugar
☐ 3 eggs
☐ 110 g self raising flour
☐ 1/4 tsp baking powder
☐ 50 g cookies and cream spread

**Decoration**
☐ 200 g butter
☐ 600 g icing sugar
☐ 2 tbsp double cream
☐ 12 cookies and cream biscuits
☐ 25 g cookies and cream crumbs

## Step 1

Preheat the oven to 170 degrees Celsius / 350 Fahrenheit/ gas mark 3. Start, by placing all your ingredients (margarine, sugar, eggs, self-raising flour) and mix them together until combined. This will loosen the batter up slightly.

## Step 2

Lastly, add in the baking powder and the cookies and cream spread the spread can make your cupcakes sink slightly so that baking powder counter reacts to that and makes them have a lovely lift.

### Step 3

Next, spoon (or use an ice cream scoop) your cupcake batter into your cupcake cases. They could be around 3/4 full for the perfect cupcake. Bake for around 22 - 25 minutes or until a cake tester or skewer inserted into the centre comes out clean.

### Step 4

Once cool, begin making your buttercream to do this mix your butter until light and fluffy. Finally, fold through your icing sugar and double cream with a drop of vanilla.

### Step 5

Once you have made your buttercream transfer to a piping bag (fitted with an open star tip) and pipe Mr Whippy by going round the edge of my cupcake over-lapping the last circling but not letting go of the pressure and when you are at the top flick of. Then, top it off with a whole cookies and cream biscuit and then some cookies and cream biscuit crumbs.

## Hints & Tips

Make sure you remember to add your extra baking powder, as this counter reacts that chunky and heavy cookies and cream spread and helps them push through and rise your cupcakes.  Once baked, make sure you leave them to cool fully else your fillings and buttercream will melt. If your buttercream is soft, or begins to soften place in the fridge for 10 minutes to firm up.

## Equipment and Ingredients

☐ 200 g dates
☐ 200 g boiling water
☐ 90 g margarine
☐ 130 g dark brown sugar
☐ 3 eggs
☐ 1 tsp mixed spice
☐ 200 g self raising flour

☐ 2 tsp Caramel flavouring

**Decoration**

☐ 200 g butter
☐ 400 g icing sugar
☐ 1 tsp caramel flavouring
☐ 50 g caramel sauce

## Step 1

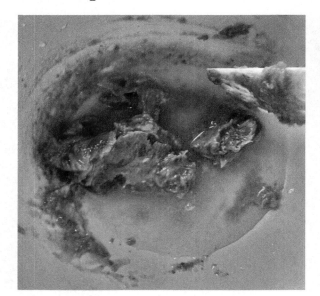

Preheat the oven to 170 degrees Celsius / 350 Fahrenheit/ gas mark 3. Start, by placing your dates (de-stoned) and blitz them until they form a paste. Use your hand blender as that blade cuts the dates up (you can use a food processor). Then, pour boiling water over the dates to loosen them up and get them to relax after all the whizzing..

## Step 2

While your whizzed up dates are relaxing, begin making the cupcakes batter which starts by beating together your butter and sugar until combined. As we are using dark brown sugar, this may take longer as the sugar needs to fully incorporated into that butter.

### Step 3

Once you have your butter and sugar combined, fold through your eggs and flour. Do not overmix at this stage as your gluten will activate in your flour and you will get a very chewy dense cupcake.

### Step 4

Finally, fold through my caramel flavouring, mixed spice and blitzed up dates. At this stage, you could add 100 g of any nuts or raisins you want (I like mine without any).

### Step 5

Finally, you need to spoon (you can use an ice cream scoop) your batter into your cupcake cases until they are around 1/2 way full. These cupcakes rise more than your normal cupcakes, so do not fill them more than 1/2 way. Then, bake for 20 minutes or until a cake tester or skewer comes out clean.

### Step 6

Now, beat together your butter, caramel flavouring and icing sugar until combined. As we are adding that caramel flavour, there no need to pre whip your butter as we don't need it to be light as that caramel coloor will react with it and turn it beige.

### Step 7

Finally, before we can eat, core out the centre of your cupcakes and fill with caramel sauce, use these centre to crush up for the topping. Transfer your buttercream to a piping bag (fitted with an open star piping tip) and pipe a rosset by starting in the centre and working my way out wrapping around as you go along. I finish with some crushed up crumbs

## Hints & Tips

Make sure your dates are fully blitzed up as you make get whole chunks of dates. When using dark brown sugar, make sure its not light brown sugar or any other sugar as it will result in a less sticky and caramelised sponge.

## Equipment and Ingredients

☐ 150 g margarine          **Decoration**

☐ 150 g caster sugar        ☐ 200 g butter

☐ 3 eggs                    ☐ 600 g icing sugar

☐ 150 g self raising flour  ☐ 12 teaspoons of jam

☐ 1/4 tsp baking powder

## Step 1

Start, by placing all your ingredients but your flour (margarine, sugar, eggs) and mix them together until combined. Then fold through your flour into the mixture This rises slightly more, because of the added baking powder as this gives you more room to scoop out your centre for the wings.

## Step 2

Next, spoon (or use an ice cream scoop) your cupcake batter into your cupcake cases. They could be around 3/4 full for the perfect cupcake. Bake for around 22 - 25 minutes or until a cake tester or skewer inserted into the centre comes out clean.

### Step 3

Once your cupcakes are cool, begin making your buttercream to do this mix your butter until light and fluffy. Finally, fold through your icing sugar and a drop of vanilla.

### Step 4

Once you have made your buttercream, scoop out the centre of your cupcakes and spoon a blob of jam into this centre and top that off with buttercream and add a little jam over the buttercream

### Step 5

Once you have added your butter-cream and jam, take the scoop that you took out and cut it in half. This forms the wings and place it either side of your jam.

## Hints & Tips

Do not overmix you batter else you will get a dense cupcake. Do not overfill your jam, or you may result in a huge puddle and your cupcake wings will not hold. You can change these to a chocolate or red velvet cupcake for a chocolate cupcake I do them the exact same chocolate cupcake chocolate buttercream sandwiched between a chocolate spread.

## Equipment and Ingredients

- ☐ 1 batch of my cupcake recipe
- ☐ 1 batch of my buttercream
- ☐ 250 g of isomalt
- ☐ red dust
- ☐ Sweet stamp perfect pour (or rejuvenator / dipping solution)
- ☐ piping bag and a open star piping tip

## Step 1

To begin with, let's start by making isomlat blood shards and to do this melt your squires kitchen isomalt (Squires kitchen is best as it doesn't go cloudy as quick as other brands). Once melted blob some onto a piece of greaseproof paper and allow to dry for 30 second.

## Step 2

After 30 seconds, mix together some dust and Sweet stamp perfect pour and take a larger paint brush and flick these onto the isomalt (if you do this before 30 seconds it may run into and cause all your isomolt to go red instead of blood splats)

## Step 3

After you have made your isomalt shard/discs. Start with taking your cupcake that you have baked using my standard cupcake recipe in a Halloween cupcake case and pipe a MR whippy out of buttercream starting from the outside and working my way up to form a mount then flicking.

## Step 4

Finally, finish by inserting the isomalt into the buttercream (you need to do this ASAP before the buttercream crusts over) and take your left over blood splatter liquid and create little pools of blood trickles on your cupcakes.

# Hints & Tips

If you want to go extra dark always make your buttercream black and this will add a more of a spooky feel. I have saw people try and use clear sweets and melt them to do this I do not recommend you will get your self in a mess and burn yourself just get a bag of squires kitchen isomalt.

## Equipment and Ingredients

- ☐ 1 batch of my cupcake recipe
- ☐ 1 batch of my buttercream recipe
- ☐ piping bag and open star piping tip
- ☐ scrumptious mermaid sprinkles
- ☐ Sprinks mermaid tail mould
- ☐ Edible art dusts
- ☐ Scrumptious lustre pumps
- ☐ Magic sparkle

# Step 1

Start, by taking around 75 g modelling paste, or flower paste ( I like a 50/50 ratio of squires kitchen and Renshaw) and placing it inside my mermaid tail mould. Then, tip it out and allow to dry. Then, dust by adding layers of different shades of colours from purples to blue to greens and pinks. Then, finish with some sparkles to make the tail bling.

# Step 2

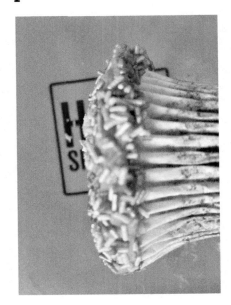

Start, with taking your cupcake that you have baked using your standard cupcakes recipe and pipe a border of buttercream (using half a batch of my simple buttercream recipe) (I dyed mine a turquoise colour) around the edge of the cupcakes.

### Step 3

Then, immediately dip this in some scrumptious sprinkles mermaid strands. (Do not allow your buttercream to crust else your sprinkles won't stick.

### Step 4

After you have stuck your sprinkles on you need to take the second half of your batch of simple buttercream and dye one half pink and one half a lilac colour and then take a pallet knife and wipe it up the side of a piping bag (fitted with an open star tip piping nozzle) so the colours are on opposite sides.

### Step 5

Once you have my two tone buttercream, then pipe around the border of that ring that has sprinkles a mini Mr Whippy in the centre and then add your mermaid tail and finish with more magic sparkles.

## Tips

Allow you mermaid tails to firm up, before placing on the cupcake to prevent them from flopping over and snapping,. Do not push your sprinkles else they will flatten the buttercream and deform the shape of the cupcake.

## Equipment and Ingredients

☐ 1 batch of my cupcake recipe

☐ 1 batch of my buttercream recipe

☐ cupcake bouquet kit (I use purple cupcakes)

☐ piping bag and a open star piping nozzle, rose petal piping nozzle and a 6b piping nozzle and GG cake craft 810 piping tip

☐ wafer paper butterfly's

☐ magic sparkle

☐ scrumptious pearls

☐ Scrumptious gold glitter pump

## Step 1

To start, making your cupcake bouquet mix your colours( I use colour mill and Sprinks colours). Dye your buttercream lilac, pink, rust and green. Then place them in the piping bags randomly make sure your green is in the 810 piping bag as this is the tip I use to create leaves.

## Step 2

Now you have your buttercream in your piping bags you can start piping. First up, you need to use the rose petal piping tip to create a ruffle. To begin, making the ruffle make sure your fat side of the nozzle is pointing up as it gives you a bigger ruffle. Then apply pressure and move you hands slowly side to side while applying pressure. Continue with all your cupcakes placing them randomly.

## Step 3

Next, we are going to make hydrangeas using our open star tip. To make the hydrangeas apply pressure and lift up it will make a Jem shape and that is your hydrangeas. Then, apply a cluster together. You also add some rosettes with this nozzle by starting in the centre of your point and wrapping the buttercream round.

## Step 4

Finally, we are going to use our 6D piping nozzle to create some texture. To do this, you need to place your piping bag just above the cupcake and move it side to side to make a swaying motion and slow it right down as you apply pressure and the buttercream comes out. You can also do a rosette with this nozzle by starting in the centre and working your way out.

## Step 5

In-between each flower I use the 810 and squeeze and pull to create some leaves. Also in-between every cupcake, add a butterfly and add some pearls. The best way to add the pearls, is using the halo sprinkles sprinkle pen. Finish with some magic sparkles and scrumptious gold glitter pump.

## Step 6

Freeze your cupcakes before placing them into tissue paper and then into your purple cupcake cupcake bouquet box.

## Hints & Tips

If your buttercream is too soft place place it in the fridge and allow it to firm up else you will end up with a melted buttercream mess. Start with pastel colours as you can not take away but you can more colours. Pastel colours look better in cupcake bouquets.

## Equipment and Ingredients

- ☐ 100 g butter
- ☐ 150 g caster sugar
- ☐ 3 eggs
- ☐ 110 g self raising flour
- ☐ 1/4 tsp baking powder
- ☐ 50 g cookies and cream spread

**Decoration**

- ☐ 200 g butter
- ☐ 600 g icing sugar
- ☐ 2 tbsp double cream
- ☐ 12 cookies and cream biscuits
- ☐ 25 g cookies and cream crumbs

## Step 1

## Step 2

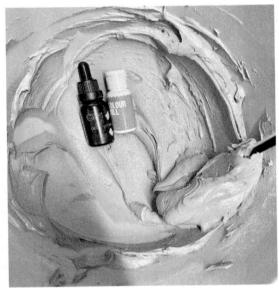

Start, by taking some yellow died flower or modelling paste (I use 50/50 Renshaw and squires kitchen) and place it into the of the large blossom mould and then place white modelling or flower paste over the top and then pop it out. Allow to firm up slightly on a apple tray to create a flower like shape.

Once you have made all 12 blossoms you take your cupcakes that you baked (using my cupcake recipe) in pastel cupcake cases and a batch of my simple buttercream died green. Next, place the buttercream into a piping bag fitted with a grass piping tip.

### Step 3

Now we are prepared and have our blossom and buttercream ready, Lets get decorating! Take your grass star nozzle and sit it onto the cake however do not push it in and then apply pressure whilst lifting up and then let go once you have your decided depth of grass. Repeat all over your cupcake.

### Step 4

Now we have our cupcakes, with grass on we can arrange the blossom, add one blossom to each cupcake. You then need to, add some Dr oketer Easter chocolate bunnies and eggs and finish with some sparkles. Do this fairly quick, else your buttercream will firm up and then your flowers will fall over and your rabbits and eggs will tip over.

## Hints & Tips

If your buttercream is to soft, place it in the fridge even in the piping bag and walk away and come back 10 minutes later and it should of firmed up. You can arrange your decorations as you wish. Remember, to allow the blossom to dry before placing it on the cupcake so they don't flop.

## Equipment and Ingredients

- ☐ 1 batch of my cupcake recipe baked in Christmas cupcake cases
- ☐ 1 batch of my buttercream recipe
- ☐ Scrumptious Christmas sprinkles (Jingle is the name of the mix I use)
- ☐ Magic sparkle

## Step 1

Take your cupcakes that you baked (using my cupcake recipe) in scrumptious mixed collection Christmas cupcake cases and a batch of your simple buttercream died green. Place the buttercream into a piping bag fitted with a open star piping tip.

## Step 2

Now you have your piping bag fitted with a open star piping tip and buttercream, take your cupcake (I prefer to have my cupcakes down on the surface as I have two hands free for the piping bag) and start on the outside building my way up like a MR whippy. Finish with, some scrumptious Christmas sprinkles and magic sparkle.

## Equipment and Ingredients

- ☐ 1 batch of my cupcakes recipe
- ☐ 1 batch of my buttercream recipe
- ☐ sweet stamp love heart sweet set
- ☐ 150 g Modelling paste (I use 50/50 Renshaw and squires kitchen)
- ☐ scrumptious sprinkles
- ☐ cake craft pink colour spray

## Step 1

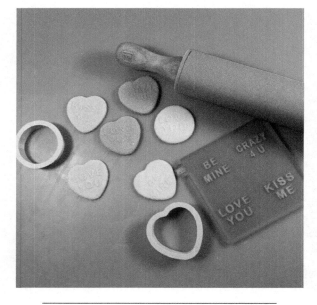

## Step 2

Start, by rolling out around 150 g of flower or modelling paste (I use 50/50 Renshaw and squires kitchen) and then take your Sweet Stamp love heart sweets embosser and push this into your coloured modelling/flower paste. Then, cut these out using the cutter in the set. Allow to dry for around 30 minutes.

Once your love hearts are dry, take your cupcakes (using my cupcake recipe) and a batch of my buttercream and pipe rosettes by starting in the centre and working your way out. I would always recommend trying on a piece of greaseproof first if its your first time so you scrape it of and try again

## Step 3

Last but not least, take your cupcakes and dip the edges in some Scrumptious mini heart sprinkles (you can use any sprinkles you want) and you make need to use your hands to push them into pace.

## Step 4

Finally, finish by adding your hearts into the centre and a little bit of magic sparkle. You can add some cake craft spray to your cupcakes (I did to add some to mine to try and bring the love through).

# Hints & Tips

You can change your dipping sprinkles, however I would stick with the Scrumptious heart sprinkles as they are amazing. You can do just one colour of modelling paste hearts and rounds. Do not, roll your hearts and rounds to thin else they won't hold and will fall over and possibility snap.

## Equipment and Ingredients

- ☐ 1 batch of buttercream
- ☐ 1 batch of cupcakes
- ☐ Edible art dusts and perfect pour (by Sweet stamp)
- ☐ Happy Sprinkles
- ☐ 25 g cookies and cream crumbs

# Step 1

# Step 2

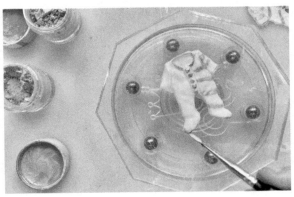

Start, by taking your modelling or flower paste (I use a blend of 50/50 Renshaw and squires kitchen) and use your Sprinks baby clothing mould to push in that flower or modelling paste and wipe of any access with your thumb. Now you have these ready, create 12 for your 12 cupcakes and allow to dry for a minimum of 6 hour preferably overnight

Once your baby clothing accessories are dry, take your Sweet stamp perfect pour liquid and mix it with your pink and blue dust to form a thin paste but not runny else it will run into the other other colours. Then, paint half off one vest blue and half off one pink and then on the baby grow pick up the main details in blue and then in pink on another (Image for reference. Finally, Allow to dry.

**Step 3**

Now, you need your batch of buttercream dye half blue and half pink use Colour mill pink and Sprinks blue.

**Step 4**

Once your buttercream is died you want to place your buttercream in a piping a bag (fitted with an open start tip) and to do this place one colour in one half and the other colour in the other half. A pallet knife will help you. Next, squeeze your buttercream down your piping bag

**Step 5**

Now you have your buttercream in your piping bag, all that is left to do is assemble. Start by piping around the outside of your cupcake and working your way up do not add to much buttercream then flick of like a Mr Whippy. Top with your mix of pink and blue sprinkles (I use happy sprinkles) and then add your modelling paste decorations and of course some magic sparkle.

## Hints & Tips

You can change the colour to a first birthday colours and paint number 1 on the vest. You need to be careful that you buttercream doesn't melt when holding it if it starts to melt place it in the fridge.

## Equipment and Ingredients

- ☐ 1 batch of my cupcake recipe
- ☐ 1 batch of my buttercream recipe
- ☐ 300 g of chocolate
- ☐ a pallet knife
- ☐ Piping bag and open star piping tip
- ☐ side scraper (I use my caking it up as it gives you more of a feather technique)

## Step 1

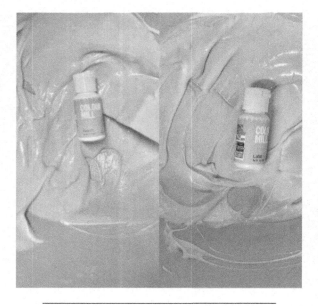

## Step 2

Start, by tempering your chocolate using your tempering guide. Use, Squires Kitchen White Chocolate and colour it with the colour mill colours. (It is very important you only use oil based colours else you will seize your chocolate as these contain water).

Spread your chocolate out onto the back of a baking tray and allow to change from a glossy shiny finish to a dull finish. Then, take the Caking it up side scraper and pull it into sections of the chocolate. This leaves a feather pattern on the chocolate. Allow to set in the fridge (this will take about 5 - 10 minutes)

## Step 3

Now you have your chocolate shard feathers, take your prebaked cupcakes and an open star tip and pipe a Mr Whippy starting on the outside and working your way up applying even pressure.

## Step 4

Now, your buttercream piped simple finish with your chocolate shard feathers. Then, top with some more magic sparkles to finish of the cupcakes.

# Hints & Tips

Change the colour of the shards to suit favourite colours. Blue and pink could be gender revel cupcakes. Add your favourite sprinkles to the cupcakes. Do not use gel food colouring or liquid else your chocolate will sizes and you have to through it away. You could also add some drizzles of chocolate over the cupcakes if you wish.

# Cookie decorating

In this chapter I show you how to take a plain sugar cookie and turn it into a party pleaser for that desert table. Every recipe starts with my basic sugar cookie recipe which I share with you.

## Equipment and Ingredients

- ☐ 140g caster sugar
- ☐ 110 ml golden or corn syrup
- ☐ 20 ml g water
- ☐ 200 g margarine
- ☐ 260 g plain flour
- ☐ 1 tbsp of your flavouring choice

# Step 1

Add your sugar, water, golden or corn syrup and butter to a saucepan and slowly bring to the boil on a medium heat. (This will take around 5 minutes as you don't want to overheat and burn you sugar)

# Step 2

Once you have your mixture boiling, take of the heat and tip in your plain flour. Bring into a ball before clingfilm and allowing to chill for 30 minutes. Once chilled preheat your oven 180 degrees roll to around the thickness of £1 and cut your shapes out then bake for around 10 minutes or until turning golden brown.

## Equipment and Ingredients

- ☐ x1 sugar cookie recipe
- ☐ bauble cookie cutter
- ☐ 250 g of sugar paste
- ☐ Scrumptious Christmas sprinkles (jingle blend)
- ☐ Magic sparkles

## Step 1

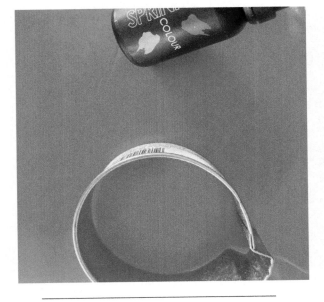

Start, by making a batch of your sugar cookie recipe and rolling to the thickness of a £1 coin then cut out your baubles using the Sprinks baubles cutter. Chill your dough for 30 minutes. Bake at 180 degrees/ 320 Fahrenheit/ gas mark 3 for 10 minutes. Once baked, allow to cool before colouring your icing red (I used Sprinks red and roll until around 3-4 mm thick and cut out you bauble shapes using your cutter.

## Step 2

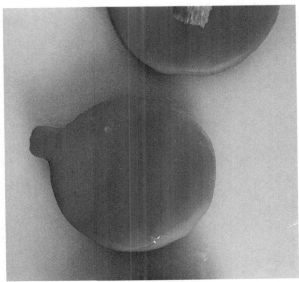

After you have cut out your sugar paste, mix together a small amount of royal icing (I use squires kitchen) to form a thin paste and paint this onto your cookies, before laying your sugar paste onto your cookie.

**Step 3**

*Once your red sugar paste is stuck down, use the royal icing around a band of the baubles to act as a glue for your sprinkles. Last. but not least, dip your baubles in the sprinkles (do not allow the royal icing to dry first). Your royal icing will be were your sprinkles stay.*

**Step 4**

*Finally, paint the top of your baubles stems with green for a little bit of contrast. Finish by adding some magic sparkle around your sprinkle band. (I use the mini Cookie countess turntable to help me decorate, and easier spin to get to every part of the cookie)*

## Hints & Tips

These Christmas bauble cookies are perfect for Christmas eve snacks or even hanging on your Christmas trees. You could do them in green if you wish and paint the top red. There are so many Christmas sprinkles out there so go wild and play with your sprinkles however these jingle sprinkles go just great.

## Equipment and Ingredients

- ☐ x1 sugar cookie recipe
- ☐ 250 g of sugar paste
- ☐ Edible art biscuit and colour mill latte
- ☐ pallet knife
- ☐ coffee cup cookie cutter

## Step 1

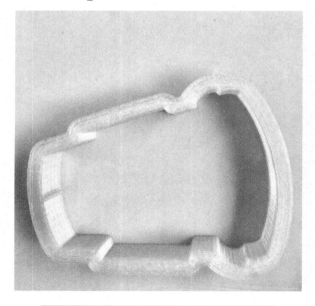

Bake a batch of my sugar cookie recipe and cut out 'The countess coffee cup cutter' (follow the guide on my sugar cookie recipe). Once baked, allow to cool before colouring your icing. I do mine in two shades of light brown one using the edible art biscuit and the other using colour mill latte. Roll both shades to around 3 - 4 mm thick.

## Step 2

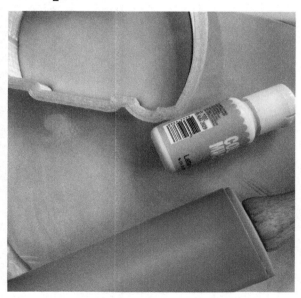

After you have cut out your whole coffee cup, take the colour mill latte shade of sugar paste and cut out the band of the coffee cup. Then, trim to size (photo for reference).

### Step 3

Once you have your coffee cup cookies and two sets of sugar paste, lets make a some royal icing. Start, by making a really runny royal icing by mixing around 50 g of Squires kitchen royal icing with 50 ml of water (this will act as a glue however you can just use edible glue, but the royal icing holds better.

### Step 4

Last but not least, paint the cookies with royal icing sticking the biscuit colour on one first then the band colour mill latte on over the top to create a 3D band.

### Step 5

Finish fine by embossing coffee into them, using the Sweet Stamp Collection. To do this, line up your letter and push them in this will create an indentation.

### Step 6

Finally, paint the top edge with royal icing and stick on some sprinkles to create an illusions there a coffee in there and your done you should have a set of brilliant coffee cups. (I use the mini Cookie countess turntable to help me decorate, and easier spin to get to every part of the cookie)

## Hints & Tips

You can change the whole colour to your colour theme, such as pink and why not use the Katy sue rose mould and add a cascade of the roses and leaves down the coffee cup. You could even add some edible images. You can even go in and paint your embossing with some edible dust and rejuvenator

## Equipment and Ingredients

- ☐ x1 batch of sugar cookie
- ☐ Sweet stamp love heart embosser and cutter set
- ☐ 150 g of sugar paste
- ☐ Squires kitchen royal icing

## Step 1

Start, by making a batch of cookies and rolling to the thickness of a £1 coin then cut out love heart and rounds using the cutters that come in the Sweet Stamp love heart sweets set. Once cut out, chill your dough for 15 minutes. Finally, bake in a preheated oven at 180 degrees/ gas mark 4 for 8 minutes.

## Step 2

Once baked, allow to cool before rolling out your sugar paste (I use sweet success) to around 3mm thick and then press in your Sweet stamp love heart embosser to emboss but pressing down. Then, cut out using the cutters in the Sweet Stamp set.

### Step 3

*Then, go over the words with gold lustre dust paint (to make this take some sweet stamp perfect pour liquid and add it to your lustre dust until you have a thick paint) a steady hand is needed.*

### Step 4

*Then, make a quick small batch of royal icing using the squires kitchen royal icing by mixing 50g of powder with 50ml of water. I use Squires Kitchen as it doesn't crust as quick as other which means you have more time to move things around.*

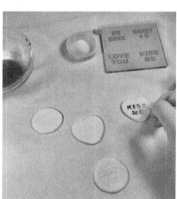

### Step 5

*Then, take your painted hearts and round cookies and add a small amount of royal icing and stick down the icing to the cookies. I then enjoyed it with a cup of coffee.*

## Hints & Tips

You could change the colour of the modelling paste or flower paste. You could change the colour from gold to something else like a silver. You could do square cookies if you have a small enough square cookie cutter.

## Equipment and Ingredients

☐ x1 batch of my cookie recipe
☐ rose and rose leaf moulds ( These are by Katy sue)
☐ 350 g modelling or flower paste ( I use 50/50 Renshaw and squires kithchen)
☐ fluted cutter ( I use purple cupcakes)
☐ magic sparkle

## Step 1

## Step 2

Bake a batch of my sugar cookie recipe and cut out the sugar cookies using the 'purple cupcakes circle cutters' (follow the guide on my sugar cookie recipe. Once baked, allow to cool. Knead your white sugar paste until smooth. Roll the white sugar paste out to around 3 - 4mm thick and use the same purple cupcake cutter to cut out the sugar paste

Then, make a quick small batch of royal icing using the squires kitchen royal icing by mixing 50g of powder with 50ml of water. Use Squires Kitchen as it doesn't crust as quick as other which means you have more time to move things around. Use this royal icing to stick down your sugar paste circles.

## Step 3

To decorate, take some Colour mill pink and Squires kitchen blue and dye 3/4 your sugar paste pink and 1/4 green (Renshaw sugar paste and place this into the Katy sue rose and leaf mould and create enough to go around the cookies.

## Step 4

Then, take more of your royal icing and paint a small amount onto the back of the leaves and roses to create a rose bush effect and place onto your cookies and finish with a little bit of magic sparkle glitter.

# Hints & Tips

You can add more or less flowers. Do not forget to cornflour your moulds else your modelling paste will get stuck in them. You could change this to different flower like blossoms and use the same concept. You could dust over the whole cookie in gold to pick up all the details.

## Equipment and Ingredients

- ☐ x1 batch of my sugar cookie recipe
- ☐ baby vest cookie cutter
- ☐ 200 g of sugar paste (I use Renshaw)
- ☐ Royal lace and knitting mat (I am using Katy sue and recommend you to)

# Step 1

# Step 2

Bake a batch of my sugar cookie recipe and cut out the sugar cookies using the 'Designer cake stencils vest cookie' (follow the guide on my sugar cookie recipe). Once baked, allow to cool before colouring your icing. I do mine in two shades one blue and one pink one ( I use Sprinks blue and Colour mill pink). Roll them both to around 3 - 4 mm thick.

Take your royal lace mat for the pink and knitted mat for the blue (I use Katy sue mats for both) and emboss them into the sugar paste a rolling pin will help you add even pressure.

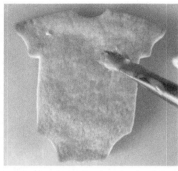

### Step 3

*We then need to make a quick small batch of royal icing, using the Squires kitchen royal icing by mixing 50g of powder with 50ml of water. I use Squires Kitchen as it doesn't crust as quick as other which means you have more time to move things around.*

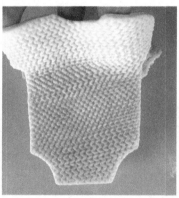

### Step 4

*Then, take your royal icing and paint a small amount onto your vest biscuit and then place on your icing. With the knitted and royal lace effect these bring the cookies to life. Finish with some magic sparkle glitter.  (I use the mini Cookie countess turntable to help me decorate, and easier spin to get to every part of the cookie)*

## Hints & Tips

You can mix and match them up with using the royal lace mat on the blue and the knitted mat on the pink. Remember, not to roll your sugar paste to thin else the mat can break through the sugar paste and leave a hole. You could add names onto them (I would use Sweet Stamp for this). If this is for a first birthday you could add the number one to each vest.

## Equipment and Ingredients

- ☐ x1 batch of my sugar cookie recipe
- ☐ 250 g sugar paste ( I use beau)
- ☐ Easter egg cutter
- ☐ Two different tones of green (I use edible art)
- ☐ paint brushes
- ☐ small amount of runny royal icing
- ☐ Big blossom mould ( I use Katy sue as they release from the moulds very easy)

## Step 1

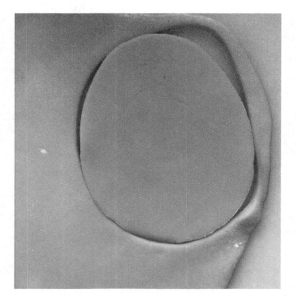

Bake a batch of my sugar cookie recipe using 'Designer cake stencils Easter egg cutter' (follow the guide on my sugar cookie recipe). Once baked, allow to cool before colouring your icing. I do mine in blue (I use squires kitchen blue). Roll the blue sugar paste to around 3- 4mm thick.

## Step 2

Once you have cut out your Easter egg sugar paste mix perfect, pour liquid (rejuvenator or dipping solution) with edible green dust. Then, take a thin paint brush and at the bottom of your egg flick it up to create a grass effect. I do the same with the white to create clouds by dabbing the white onto the top of the blue sugar paste.

## Step 3

Then, take my Katy sue big blossom mould and use the smaller blossom and a small amount of yellow sugar paste and place these into the centre. I back them of with white sugar paste. Tip them out your mould and allow to dry slightly for around 10 minutes.

## Step 4

We then need to make a quick small batch of royal icing using the Squires Kitchen royal icing by mixing 50g of powder with 50ml of water. I use Squires Kitchen as it doesn't crust as quick as other which means you have more time to move things around.

## Step 5

Then, take your royal icing and paint a small amount onto your Easter egg biscuit and then place on your icing. Then, apply a small amount of royal icing on the back of the blossom to stick this down. Place these in the top right hand corner. Then, finish with a little bit of magic sparkle. (I use the mini Cookie countess turntable to help me decorate, and easier spin to get to every part of the cookie)

# Hints & Tips

I use blossoms you could use any other flower you like. I do the grass in just greens however you could incorporated some white. The changes you can do are endless you could even add white parallel down the whole side of one of the cookies.

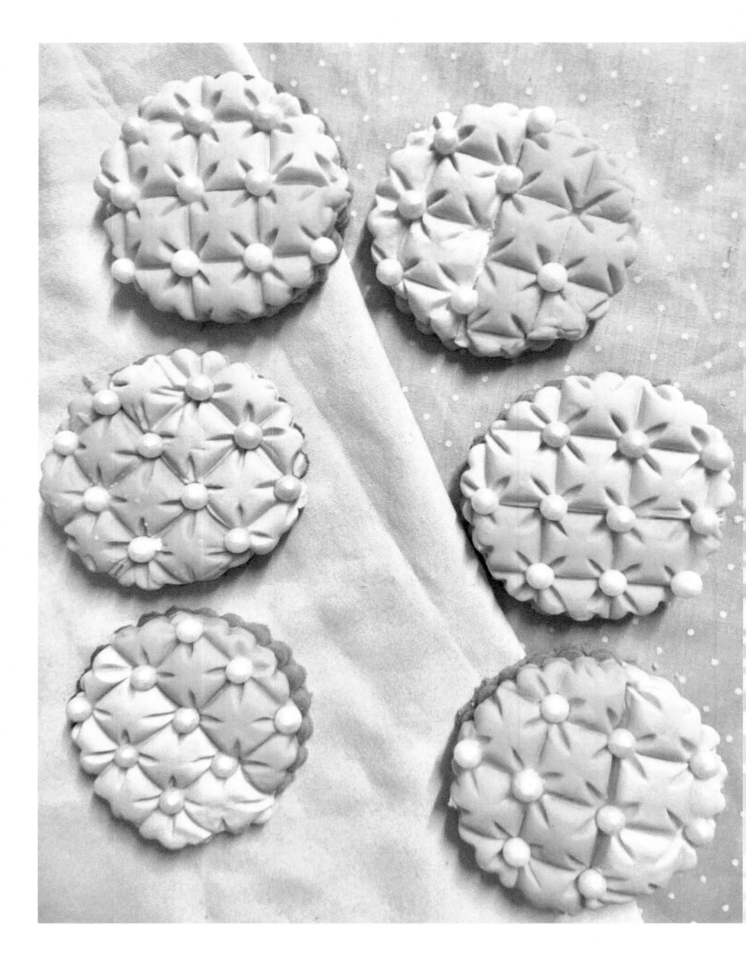

## Equipment and Ingredients

- ☐ x1 batch of my sugar cookie recipe
- ☐ continuous quilting mould (I love the Katy sue moulds)
- ☐ fluted cutter  (Purple cupcakes are great as they have the sizes on the cutter)
- ☐ Scrumptious pearls
- ☐ 250 g sugar paste

## Step 1

## Step 2

Bake a batch of my sugar cookie recipe using 'Purple cupcake circle cutter' (follow the guide on my sugar cookie recipe. Once baked, allow to cool before colouring your icing. I do mine in blue and pink  (I use Squires kitchen blue and colour mill blush). Roll both blue and pink sugar pastes into your Katy sue continuous quilting mould.

Dust your Katy sue mould with icing sugar or cornflour. Roll over your Katy sue mould using a rolling pin. Then use a 3cm purple cupcake cutter and use the fluted side to cut them out. Then, use the marks to cut in half.

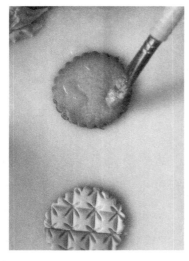

## Step 3

We then need to make a quick small batch of royal icing, using the Squires Kitchen royal icing by mixing 50g of powder with 50ml of water. I use Squires Kitchen as it doesn't crust as quick as other which means you have more time to move things around. (I use the mini Cookie countess turntable to help me decorate, and easier spin to get to every part of the cookie)

## Step 4

Then, take your royal icing and paint a small amount onto your fluted biscuit and then place on your icing. Then, go in-between the crevasse and place a scrumptious pearl. Finish, with some magic sparkle glitter.

## Tips

You can flavour the biscuit any flavour you want. You can colour the icing any colour you wish. You can change the colour and size of your pearls. Remember to add cornflour or icing sugar to you mould to avoid your sugar paste sticking.

# Celebration cakes

In this chapter I take my back to basic sponge recipe and turns them into amazing cakes for the likes of birthday and baby showers.

## Equipment and Ingredients

- ☐ x2 sponge cakes
- ☐ x1 batch of buttercream
- ☐ sprinkles (I use a mix of purple cupcakes, happy sprinkles and scrumptious)
- ☐ pallet knife
- ☐ cake scraper
- ☐ Cake craft USA drip

## Step 1

To begin the cake, make my sponge cake recipe. Then, cut the crust of the top of your sponges and then cut them in half. Then, use a purple cupcake 3cm cutter and cut each sponge. I start by pushing the circle cutter roughly in the centre roughly then use the above tier as a guide to cut the rest so there even. Remember to keep the bottom one free so your sprinkles don't fall out.

## Step 2

Then, layer them up, you can buttercream or jam between your layers (I don't as I think it can make it wobbly, however,  you can add dowels to make it more stable). Then, fill the cakes with a mixture of sweets and sprinkles (or what ever you wish to). Top with your cut out circle.

**Step 3**

Apply, a layer of buttercream as a crumb coat so we have something for our sprinkles to stick to. Apply, this using a pallet knife and scrape it of using a cake scraper as we want a very thin layer of buttercream.

**Step 4**

Last but not least, place your own blends of sprinkles into a tray (I use the halo sprinkle tray) and then use your hands to push the sprinkles up the cake and on top of the cake. This bit is very messy.

**Step 5**

Finish, by adding a drip (I use Cake craft USA drip). Add a small amount of colour mill blush to create a gorgeous pink and place the drip into a piping bag so I have more control and drip. Finish with, a half batch of my buttercream in a piping bag fitted with a open star tip. Pipe mini Mr Whippys and finish with confetti sprinkles.

## Tips

I wouldn't recommend moving this cake once you have inserted your sprinkles, else they may fall out if you layers slide. You can change your drip colours your sprinkle theme and your inside surprise, you could add money toys or anything you want. Do not pick your cake up and roll in sprinkles use your hands else again your sprinkles will fall out the inside. Remember to add your sprinkles while your buttercream is soft else they will not stick to the buttercream.

## Equipment and Ingredients

- ☐ x1 batch of sugar cookie dough
- ☐ x1 batch of buttercream
- ☐ 200 g white chocolate
- ☐ piping bag
- ☐ Open star piping tip

## Step 1

Start, by making a batch of my sugar cookies and printing our your desired number or shape recipe and rolling to a thickness just over a £1 coin then cut out your shape using your template. Once cut out, chill your dough for 30 minutes. Finally, bake in a preheated oven at 180 degrees/ gas mark 4 for 15 minutes or until golden brown

## Step 2

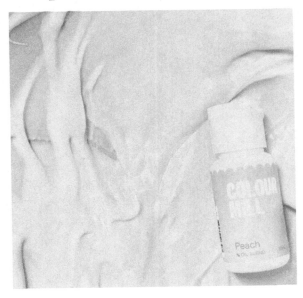

Whilst your cookie letter or number is cooling, use my tempering guide to temper some white chocolate (I use Squires kitchen) and then colour the chocolate using Colour mill and place it into a mini bar mould ( I use Sprinks) and allow to set in the fridge for around 10 minutes.

**Step 3**    *Whilst your chocolate is setting make a batch of my simple buttercream. Take half of this and dye it pink and fit it in a piping bag fitted with a 6B piping tip. Take the other half and add some white food colouring to turn it bright white and place that in a open piping bag.*

**Step 4**    *Finally, take your piping nozzle and pipe on your base cookie. Pipe blobs of jems (using the pink buttercream by applying pressure then letting go but twisting as you let go. Then, use the white putting cream to pipe white hydrangers by applying pressure and letting go.*

**Step 5**    *Finally, top with some dusted gold macrons and your chocolate bars and some happy sprinkles. You can add more toppings if you wish.*

## Tips

Go light on the colour, to begin with as pastel colours work better for this sugar cookie number/letter. Follow my tempering guide for the chocolate. At any point if your buttercream becomes soft, leave it in the fridge even in the piping bags for 15 minutes then come back and go again.

## Equipment and Ingredients

- ☐ x2 sponge cakes
- ☐ 1 batch of buttercream
- ☐ pro froster
- ☐ piping bag and piping nozzle
- ☐ pallet knife
- ☐ fresh or artifical flowers

## Step 1

Take your cakes and start levelling them using my levelling guide. You want to now start layering the cakes and adding buttercream in-between each layer. To do this take your bottom layer of cake and place it on a board and then take a piping bag of buttercream and pipe a ring. Now you want to place your filling in this ring. Place your above layer on top and repeat with the other layers.

## Step 2

Once your cake is layered up, you want to take your remaining buttercream and apply this to the top and the sides using a pallet knife. Then, take a scraper and scrape it of until you can see the cake coming through but you have a small amount of buttercream on the outside.

### Step 3

Now, you have your crumb coat you want to place this in the fridge to firm up. Now repeat the crumb coat steps to make sure the cake is fully crumb coated to stop the air drying it out. Repeat with the above tier if you wish to (use my dowelling guide to see how to stack your cake).

### Step 4

Finish by adding some flowers. To do this you will need to add them to posy picks to make sure there food safe and remove them before easting. Simple insert the flower into the posy picks and insert the posy pick into your cake and you will now need to get arranging your flowers as you wish.

## Tips

You can flavour your sponge to which ever flavour you want even add some raspberries or blueberries to your sponge so it pops through your crumb coat of buttercream. Change your buttercream colours to suit your theme. Do not scrape of all your buttercream else the air exposed to your cake will make your cake dry.

## Equipment and Ingredients

- ☐ x2 chocolate cakes (8 inch's)
- ☐ 2 batch of chocolate buttercream
- ☐ pro froster
- ☐ piping bag and piping nozzle
- ☐ pallet knife
- ☐ piping bag and open star piping nozzle
- ☐ Scrumptious gold pump
- ☐ Hazelnut truffles
- ☐ magic sparkles

# Step 1

# Step 2

Take your cake and level them (using my levelling guide). Now let's start stacking the cakes and adding chocolate buttercream in-between each layer. To do this take your bottom layer of cake and place it on a board and then place a dollop of buttercream and smooth it out evenly using a pallet knife.

Once your layers are stacked, you want to take your remaining chocolate buttercream and apply this to the top and the sides using a pallet knife. Apply, a very thick layer and use your Profroster to smooth this out all the access will come of.

### Step 3

Place nuts around the bottom of the cake, using your hand to push them in is the best way to make sure there stuck in.

### Step 4

After you have have added your nuts, bring your double cream to the boil either in the microwave or over a pan of simmering water. Pour over your chocolate. Set aside for 15 minutes to cool.

### Step 5

While your ganahe is cooling freeze your cake this stops your drip from running everywhere and will set the drip.

### Step 6

Once your ganache has cooled slightly, pour over the top of your cake and use the pallet knife to edge the drip down your cake.

### Step 7

Finish, by transferring your remaining buttercream into a piping bag (fitted with an open star piping tip) and pipe little Mr Whippys by starting in the centre and working your way up. Top with some hazelnut truffles and some scrumptious gold glitter and of course some magic sparkles.

## Tips

You can change the flavour of your sponge to a vanilla sponge if you did not want the cake so chocolatey. You could always change your nuts from hazelnuts to walnuts. You could always use walnut truffles on top. If you want a thicker drip make your cake cold so it sets the drip while it dripping so it doesn't run down the whole cake.

# Children's baking

Have you always wanted to bake with the children or grandchildren and do not know what to bake, as there to recipes many to chose from or your children might get bored after 100 steps that's what this chapter has solved helping you make quick and easy bakes.

## Equipment and Ingredients

- ☐ 70g margarine
- ☐ 150 g milk chocolate
- ☐ 3 eggs
- ☐ 5 tbsp of golden syrup
- ☐ 140 g of cornflakes
- ☐ Scrumptious mini eggs

## Step 1

Start, by melting your butter, chocolate and syrup until it forms a liquid. Do not overheat this mixture, else you may burn your chocolate. While this is melting, line my cupcake tray with cupcake cases

## Step 2

Simply , pour into your cupcake cases and make sure you evenly distributed your mixture and top with some scrumptious mini eggs and refrigerate for around 2 hours or until set.

## Equipment and Ingredients

- ☐ 125g margarine
- ☐ 125 g caster sugar
- ☐ 125 g self raising flour
- ☐ 3 eggs
- ☐ 250 g butter
- ☐ 250 Icing sugar
- ☐ Scrumptious sprinkles

## Step 1

Preheat the oven to 160 degrees Celsius/ gas mark 3/ 320 Fahrenheit. Start, by mixing together your butter, sugar, eggs, flour and raspberry flavouring until it comes together to form a batter. The batter should not be runny but should not be that thick when it held on a spatula it doesn't fall of after 10 seconds

## Step 2

To portion your ice cream cone cases place them onto a baking sheet and use two spoons or place your cupcake batter into a piping bag and place your mixture into your ice cream cones. There is a rim below the top rim on the cones and fill the batter to that rim. Then, bake in my preheated oven for 20 - 22 minutes or until cooked.

## Step 3

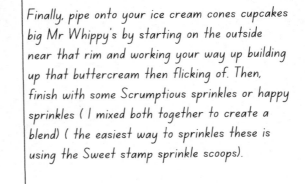

Next, beat your butter until light and fluffy (I use a hand mixer but you can do this by hand.) Once your butter is light and fluffy fold through your icing sugar and mix again. Transfer to a piping bag fitted with an open star piping nozzles.

## Step 4

Finally, pipe onto your ice cream cones cupcakes big Mr Whippy's by starting on the outside near that rim and working your way up building up that buttercream then flicking of. Then, finish with some Scrumptious sprinkles or happy sprinkles ( I mixed both together to create a blend) ( the easiest way to sprinkles these is using the Sweet stamp sprinkle scoops).

## Tips

You can colour your buttercream to any colour you wish. You can change the flavour add more decorations or less. You could change the sprinkles. If the buttercream gets to hot place place the buttercream in the before continuing.

## Equipment and Ingredients

- ☐ 1 batch of my cupcakes
- ☐ 1 batch of my buttercream
- ☐ Piping bag and grass piping nozzle
- ☐ 15 mini cookies
- ☐ Edible sugar eyes

# Step 1

# Step 2

Start, by colouring you buttercream in a very light shade of blue (I recommend using Sprinks blue). Then, transfer this to a piping bag fitted with a grass piping tip.

Take your cupcake and use your buttercream in the piping bag and go around the cupcake and squeezing and lifting up. Once you go all over the cupcake, dangle the nozzle and squeeze and this will add a more rustic effect. Finish, with some edible eyes and half a mini cookie for the mouth.

## Equipment and Ingredients

- ☐ 200 g margarine
- ☐ 300 g light brown sugar
- ☐ 3 eggs
- ☐ 75 g plain flour
- ☐ 55 g cocoa powder
- ☐ 150 g  milk chocolate
- ☐ speculose sauce
- ☐ caramelised biscuit

## Step 1

Start, by melting your chocolate by it self until it's flows smoothly.. You can do this in a bain-marie (Saucepan of simmering water with a bowl over the top) or short burst in the microwave. Set aside to cool down.

## Step 2

Beat together you butter and sugar until fully incorporated you want this to almost double in size. This will take about 5 minutes.

### Step 3

Next, fold in your cocoa powder, eggs and flour until fully combined this should form a loose paste.

### Step 4

Finally, fold in your melted chocolate make sure you don't have some areas with more chocolate than the other. Do not overbeat else all the air you created with that butter and sugar will disappear so your bronuts won't be light and fluffy.

### Step 5

Pipe into your donut mould and bake in your preheated oven for 25 - 35 minutes depending if you want your brounuts more cakey or fudgy. Allow to cool fully.

### Step 6

Once your bronuts have cooled drizzle with some speculoos sauce and top with a caramelised biscuit and crumbs of a crushed up biscuit.

## Tips

You must not overbeat the batter as all the air you created with the butter and sugar will collapse. Be careful with your chocolate and keep checking it as if your chocolate burns you will need to bin the whole batch there is no way back from burnt chocolate.

## Equipment and Ingredients

- ☐ 200 g marshmallows
- ☐ 75 g margarine
- ☐ 200 g rice krispies
- ☐ Scrumptious sprinles

# Step 1

Start, by melting together your margarine and marshmallows. You can do this, in a sauce or microwave. To stir the butter and marshmallows, grease a spatula and stir so the marshmallows do not stick. Be aware in the saucepan they will caramelise slightly.

# Step 2

Fold together your marshmallow and butter, with your sprinkles and rice krispy's. Place, into a foil tray. Refrigerate overnight and then it will pop out your foil tray (if you are using normal baking tins you will need to line these to hep you get them out).

# Brands I recommend

## Beau products

I recommend beau products mainly for there flavouring they also do sugar paste which is easy to work with and covers cake like a dream. Scan the QR code to be taken to there website www.beauproducts.co.uk

## Happy sprinkles

Happy sprinkles do an amazing range of vibrant sprinkle that perfect for topping your cakes and cupcakes. Scan the QR code to be taken to there website www.happysprinkles.com

## Edible Art

Edible art do a wide range of edible dusts from matte dusts to lustre dusts and they are great for dusting chocolates to dusting cakes. Scan the QR code to be taken to there website www.edableartworldofcolour.co.uk

# Squires Kitchen

I can not recommend Squires kitchen enough they put bakers at the heart of what they are doing and every product is excellent. Scan the QR code to be taken to Squires Kitchen Instgram page

# Katy Sue

The best of the best Katy sue mould's are one of the best ranges of moulds you can pick up. Scan the QR code to be taken to there website www.katysue.com

# Colour Mill

If you are after chocolate colours that are true to colour these are the ones to buy every colour in there range are so vibrant and easy to match on the bottle. Scan the QR code to be taken to there website www.colourmill.com.au

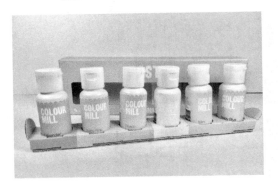

# Sweet Stamp

Sweet Stamp have a whole host of products from there best in the business sweet stamps to there trendy rolling pin Scan the QR code to be taken to there website www.sweetstamp.online

# Select Ireland

Select Ireland offer s premium sugar paste that nor only easy to use but value for money and if you buy select Ireland there is less chance your sugar paste will tear as it a quality sugar paste. Scan the QR code to be taken to there website www.selectfoods.ie

# Scrumptious

Scrumptious Sprinkles have a wide range of sprinkles that are bake stable including there confetti pack. Scan the QR code to be taken to there website www.scrumptious.uk.net

# Sweet Success

Sweet success offer premade cakes for those stressful weeks with lots of wedding cakes or birthday cakes. But my favourite product is there sugar paste. It white in colour and tastes delicious. Scan the QR code to be taken to there website www.sweetsuccess.uk.com

# Little pod

Scrumptious Sprinkles have a wide range of sprinkles that are bake stable including there confetti pack. Scan the QR code to be taken to there website www.littlepod.co.uk

# Dr Oetker

Dr Oetker is a supermarket and household baking name here in the UK from there fabulous baking powders to chocolate decorations and cocoa powder there a product to please you. Scan the QR code to be taken to there website www.oetker.co.uk

# Olbaa

Strong cake boards and boxes perfect for displaying your cakes. Scan the QR code to be taken to there website
www.olbaa.uk

# Magic sparkles

Magic sparkles are the best sparkles you can get for your take as they really bling in your face. There no trying to find the light to catch them they really sparkle. Scan the QR code to be taken to there website
www.magicsparkle.com

# Mosser glass

The go to cake stand company with a whole range of colours there cake stands have to be the best. Scan the QR code to be taken to there website
www.mosserglass.com

# Wright flour

I use Wright flour for all my baking it gives them a good rise and the quality overall of the flour is very good.
www.wrightsbaking.co.uk

# Acknowledgements

Caking it better has been a combination of my lifetime of caking knowledge and there are a few main people that I need to thank for allowing me to bring this book to life and the main one is you guys those of you who has purchase a copy and supported me on the journey. I would not be hear without you.

Secondly, all the companies that put there faith into me from sending out products to sending me motivational messages. I felt your support from the minute I put my idea in front of you.

Thirdly, the printer and manufacture of Caking it better. I want to thank you for allowing me to have the idea of creating a second book.

Lastly, my family for allowing me to hog the kitchen for endless our and get in your way why your trying to cook tea. Allowing me to chat your head of about the book.

If you have enjoyed this book as much as I did creating it and want to share your recreations check out my social media using the @Sweetsugarlayers

Printed in Great Britain
by Amazon